The Book of Light

Pat Grieco

Other Books by Pat Grieco

The Art of Nauga Farming

Compulsion

Rhetoric

First Print Edition

Print edition produced in the United States of America

Cover Photo Art: Pat Grieco
Illustrations: Pat Grieco

Print ISBN: 978-1-7324688-0-1

Pen and Lute
www.penandlute.com

The final approval for this literary material is granted by the author.

Library of Congress Control Number: 2018966719

Distributed Publication
Lexington, KY
Middletown, DE
San Bernardino. CA

DEDICATION

For those who ask the difficult questions

The Book of Light

Pat Grieco

Grieco

God blessed the devil every day
in hopes that he'd reform,
knowing really all along
his hopes were quite forlorn.
The devil surely had his goals
t'were not the same as God's
and so the two would always be
eternally at odds.

I have a body but I am not my body.
I have a mind but I am not my mind.
I have emotions but I am not emotion.
I am the other,
the essence that exists beyond the dark
growing in understanding and being.

Contents

Foreword...1
Interrogatory 3
The Meaning of Life 4
The Lion...5
Let there be… 8
Time, Evolution, and the Growing God 15
    Time..15
    Evolution..16
    Metaphysical Evolution 19
    Paradox and the Growing God 20
    Multiverse and meta-universe...........................23
Another Round..28
Reality..35
A Conversation 41
A Question of Faith 50
Another Conversation..57
Of Good and Evil...63
Old Wisdom...72
Prelude to Understanding 74
Memory..77
Faith – Knowledge – Choice 80
The coming season 82
The Sky Is Blue Today 85
Doctrine 86
I Stand Alone 91
Understanding..95
Prayers from a heretic 98
Thoughts Cast Upon the Face of Eternity...........104
Prayer of the Discontent 106
Dialogue...108
Belief..111
The Heavens Wept..112
Epilog...116
Acceptance...118

The Book of Light

Postscript...119
List of Illustrations...123

Foreword

In each lifetime, we gain experience in the practical realities of life. We learn about the basic scientific "truths" that govern the universe. We get exposed to the philosophies, religious and otherwise, that attempt to make sense of existence. Yet regardless of all we know, or think we know, none of us can really be sure what comes next, what follows the brief moment of consciousness of each human life.

We start with the fact that we exist, that all life, indeed all things come from somewhere, something, and ultimately move from here to some other state of existence. But it is here that we differ in our knowledge, in our beliefs, in our understanding of all that is, all that has been, and all that will ever be.

Each, in our own way, deals with the concepts of creation, free choice, predestination, sentience, morality, reincarnation, evolution, heaven, hell, nirvana, or the abyss of nothingness. All are encompassed in our cultures, our religions, our science, and our personnel beliefs.

It is how we define these things that determines how we live. Those definitions are determined by how we understand the physical and metaphysical building blocks of life. Within those definitions, it is our choices that enlighten or confine us in beliefs, in structured paths that mark the boundaries between a worthwhile life and one thought less, between good and evil, between the light and the dark.

Our view of what the meaning of life is depends on who we are, how we have been raised, our choices, and those made by others all around us. It is as simple or as complex as we choose to make it and often changes as we age and gain knowledge and understanding. But ultimately, all that we think we know, all that we think we understand may be wrong. And ultimately, what we think, what we believe, may be completely unimportant.

Interrogatory

What if I had never fallen?

Who then would be your whipping boy as you work your evil in his name? At least I was honest in my choice, admitting freely to my ends with full understanding and acceptance of the cost and consequences.

You. You delude yourself, doing things that if done by others would be considered "my" work. But in your heart you know, even as you talk of reward and punishment in the name of good.

But there is no reward, for there is none to give beyond what you have now. There is no punishment, for the irony is that you do this to yourself and no punishment could be greater than this. There is only one good and you know nothing of it.

I see you do not understand. Perhaps that is for the best. For if you understood you would have to choose. If you chose you would have to act. Once you act you can no longer be indifferent regardless of whether you hide in plain sight or move to right the endless wrongs of an imperfect world.

Stripped of indifference can you ever truly be satisfied with less than knowing, with less than seeing all that is, as it is, in all the shades of truth, in all the varieties of light and darkness?

What if I had never fallen?

The Meaning of Life

The meaning of Life is to defeat entropy and stop the endless downward flow of energy in order to permit, allow, enable continued existence in a stable, energy continuum.

The meaning of Life is to transcend human mortality, embrace the spiritual essence of existence and achieve oneness with God.

There is no meaning of Life. You are born, you exist, and you die. You should hope for nothing more than this.

Which one do you believe in? It's alright. You can answer honestly. Only you will know which one you've chosen.

Got one? Good. It doesn't matter which one you've selected. You are both correct and wrong in whatever choice you've made.

None of the three statements is completely correct by themselves. By the same measure none of them by themselves is completely wrong.

The three statements are three parts of the same answer to the question "What is the meaning of Life?"

No matter how hard we try to separate them, to make them three separate views of life, of existence, they are in fact inseparable.

Science, metaphysics, mortality, all part of a single whole; three facets of existence which begin with Light.

The Lion

From the heavens all aglow,
two stars blazed down on Earth below
    where stood the Lion.

One could tell with just a glance,
it was not luck or merely chance
that these two stars should come to dance
    where stood the Lion.

The stars, they hovered in the air,
emitting such a frightful glare,
that even shadows could not dare
    stand near the Lion.

"'Twas for fear the shadows fled."
whispered many in their dread
and still on all the Light was shed
    from near the Lion.

"No, I think it was from fright
the shadows quickly took to flight."
said those turning from the Light
    above the Lion.

"It was not fear, it was not fright,
that drove the shadows from the Light."
came a statement from the right
    beyond the Lion.

All there turned to see a man,
standing tall, quite trim and tan.
All there saw him place one hand
    upon the Lion.

"The Light is truth, as all can see.
No shadows of deceit could possibly
exist, when once truth is set free
    as by the Lion."

"Nonsense," cried a man in black,
"that statement merely shows his lack,
the lights are not what's true, in fact
    it is the Lion."

Lo the shadows grew and rose
to encircle all of those
standing, straining on their toes
    to see the Lion.

"Do not believe the Light is true."
said the man now dressed in blue.
"That man has merely lied to you.
    Truth is the Lion."

Again, the tall, trim man stood forth.
"The Light is true." again he taught.
But now the man in blue grew wroth.
    "Truth is the Lion!"

"Stone him! Kill him!" came a yell.
Just from where, no one could tell.
Nonetheless that man was felled
    there by the Lion.

No one in the crowd could say
just how they came to kill that day
as they knelt in dark to pray
    before the Lion.

So they come from near and far,
some by foot, some by car,
most of them ignored the stars
and worshipped, the now unbarred
    Lion.

Let there be...

Light. It all begins with Light. The Big Bang, the Creation stories, the first spark of conception. We all know it. It's inherent in our understanding of who we are, how we got here, and where, if anyplace, we're going. Yet before there was Light there was still something, something for that Light to act against, react against, and exist within. We are taught that Light is the beginning and that it is, was, shall be for all of existence, for all of time as it were. If we accept this as our starting point, all else follows.

So what existed before the Big Bang? What was it that the Light exists within? Since everything we know begins with the instant of creation, we can define what was before as the absence of all that came to be, or nothingness, a void as it were. This Void can be characterized as an endless, changeless expanse of eternity, empty and undistinguished within itself. Yet somehow, somewhere, sometime, a spark of something appears in the Void. This presents us with a basic paradox. Because it appears in unchanging eternity, although it had a beginning, this spark was always there. And yet, as that spark appears, time begins and with it the struggle for existence. Everything that ever was, is, or shall be, begins at that instant, existing simultaneously within the Void.

It is a strong, yet simple concept, that all of existence is contained within something else. That if you somehow stood within the Void/Eternity, you could examine all of existence with Time laid out like a map on a table, easy to look at but perhaps difficult to understand without getting into the details. If we accept that all we are originated with that first spark, then all physical and metaphysical laws can be traced to the beginning of existence. With that as our starting point, we can extrapolate backwards in our attempt to understand the reason for, the need for creation, and the evolutionary path, the momentum that in one instance has resulted in us.

A Void can be considered to be a perfect or pure vacuum. It is a system devoid of energy in any of its forms or states (e.g., light or matter without any of the interactions thereof). Prevailing thought seems to be that such a perfect vacuum cannot exist or be manufactured within the space-time environment as it would serve as a powerful attractant for energy. At some point, energy would leak into the vacuum from the space-time environment thus compromising its integrity as a non-energy system.

For our purposes, let's say that this non-energy system, an all-encompassing Void, did exist. As a non-energy system, it would be unchanging and thus timeless and eternal from a perspective inside it. Perhaps the Void existed as either a fundamental natural state or as a manufactured system using technologies we are, as of yet, unaware. The difference might seem small. But one could see it as the difference between a space-time environment driven by creation from a God entity and an artificial construct resulting from the complex interactions of energy governed by fundamental laws.

In either case, the introduction of energy into a non-energy (perfect vacuum/Void) system could have dramatic results. Provided the integrity of the perfect vacuum remained intact, one could suppose that something akin to the "Big Bang" would be the result. Within the bubble of the perfect vacuum, the introduced energy could be supposed to expand at an exponential rate from the point of origin.

Regardless of the "actual" size of the Void, from inside, it would, for all practical purposes, be infinite. Thus, the expansion of energy would perhaps never fill it. Over time, the energy would become more diffuse and scattered as it moved outward from the point of origin. One manifestation associated with the introduction of energy into the Void is what we have come to call light, a byproduct of complex interactions within our space-time environment.

Over the course of human history, the term "light" has come to be defined in scientific terms as a particular form of electromagnetic radiation found along the broader expanse of the electromagnetic spectrum. But "light" has also acquired another meaning associated with metaphysical matters. It has come to be associated with the battle of good against evil, with light being associated with the good whereas evil is associated with the dark or the absence of "the light". To distinguish the origin energy, (that first spark), from electromagnetic radiation and to provide a common reference point for metaphysical discussion, let's call this origin energy "Light."

Thus somehow, somewhere, "sometime", a spark of Light appeared in the Void. As such, the Light was in an endless vacuum and, like in the theory of the "Big Bang", could be supposed to have started to expand to fill that infinite, eternal Void. The appearance of Light in the Void can be thought of as the moment of creation. However, barring a belief in the instantaneous creation of the universe in its present form, with nature and Humanity a result of intelligent design, our thoughts on what occurred thereafter are shaped, in some measure, by some variation of one of the following three creation views.

In the first, the Light is just energy and all that results from its introduction into the Void is due to the random combination of events culminating in the universe and ourselves. Somehow the Light did more than just expand into the Void. It exploded into the Void with all that followed simply a result of physical laws and interactions.

The second view is very close to the first with the exception that the explosion of the Light into the Void culminates in a material universe governed by both physical and metaphysical laws and interactions.

The third view differs from the first two in an important detail. Perhaps the Light was sentient. Perhaps it came to understand what was happening to it. In this view, if it had not, you would not be reading this, for it would have simply continued to expand becoming more and more diffuse until it essentially ceased to be. In this view, for some reason, (survival?), the Light changes. It creates from its own substance. And from that creation comes the physical and metaphysical universe we are familiar with, the one we think we know.

It's probably fair to say that no one really knows what would happen if one managed to introduce energy into a stable perfect vacuum. However, the appearance of Light in the Void could be considered the "Big Bang", with the inevitable expansion outward across eternity. For some, it is viewed as marking the appearance, the emergence of God, for it is from this Light that all else comes. However, along with the "Big Bang" and the subsequent expansion and evolution of the universe also comes the onset of mortality. For up until a certain point in evolution, all things fail, returning to a lower level of energy in the struggle against entropy, the fight to survive.

The amount of energy required to create the elemental matter that forms at the birth of the universe is staggering even to contemplate. Yet in that moment of creation, of birth, the possibility of survival is assured. The concept of evolution underpins all three views of creation. In the first two, the evolving universe is merely the result of physical and perhaps metaphysical processes. The third view of creation holds that, having been created of the sentient Light, each speck, each sub-atomic particle and atom is imbued with a fragment of consciousness. In a sense dormant, these fragments are nonetheless linked in a universal net that provides the background force, the material for evolution to work with.

In all three views, all that we are is a result of evolution, that fight to slowly build up and sustain energy as reflected in physical and organic matter. In views two and three we add metaphysical constructs to the mix. In the beginning, we have rapidly expanding clouds of charged particles and matter, superheated but cooling rapidly as they move away from the point of origin. Yet even as this mass of elemental gas and particles begin their expansion, they also begin the process of concentration, of collecting together to form other, more complex material structures. These structures grow still larger and more complex, gathering essence and matter together until stars are born with accompanying planets and smaller objects emerging from the ordered chaos of the expanding universe.

In a sense we have a kind of material evolution, a stabilization and reversal of the dispersion into the Void, building from less complex arrangements of particles and atoms to more dense combinations of matter. In the first view of creation, this is all you get. Everything that is, is a result of these physical interactions of matter and energy. In the second and third views, one could infer that some forms of these material structures become self-aware as matter becomes more complex and dense in nature. Packing that elemental stuff together, with the essence that is integral to each being woven together as well, might just provide the metaphysical opportunity for a form of life, of consciousness to emerge. But although we have anthropomorphized everything from rocks to the sun, our understanding of what constitutes life does not include the potential that inorganic matter, if complex enough, might somehow be alive. And, regardless of how we view that possibility, there is only so much matter and therefore perhaps a limit to the degree of complexity a purely inorganic material evolution could achieve.

In all three views, humans have very strong opinions on what being alive means, with all of them centered on organic-based existence. It's a very Earth-centric view focused on the emergence of the first speck of organic matter. Prior to that instant, there was no distinction in terms of matter. After that moment, everything changes with organic matter beginning its long march uphill from organic soup and compounds to cells and organisms to complex creatures and beings living upon and within the structures of the inorganic universe. With the emergence of organic matter, we arrive at a point where evolution is not constrained by the limits on inorganic matter. Instead, we now add to the complexity of matter present in the universe as organic matter grows and replicates itself and evolves into new and more intricate organisms. Each link, each combination of organic structures is a piece in the evolutionary chain stretching back to the Light.

Without the Light there is no matter. Without matter there is no Universe. Without the Universe and its systems of galaxies, each with their stars and planets, there is no suitable place for organic matter and ultimately life, as we recognize it, to emerge. Each plays its part in the evolutionary process leading to the development, the emergence of more and more complexity in the physical realm.

This evolution of complexity encompasses the metaphysical realm in the second and third views of creation. In the second, metaphysical evolution is sparked somewhere along the chain of material evolution. In the third, everything, at the instant of creation, contains a corresponding speck of consciousness. With each increase in material and organic complexity, a matching increase in the complexity of that metaphysical consciousness also occurs. In both views, when the complexity, the density of that consciousness reaches a threshold level, the conditions exist for the continuance of the metaphysical form beyond the ending of the host structure. Once that evolutionary threshold is passed, the stage is set for the emergence of a continuing metaphysical entity, or as we call it – the soul.

Time, Evolution, and the Growing God

Time

Time is essentially the measurement of change in eternity. When the Light/Big Bang appeared in the Void, change was introduced into a static environment. One can measure that change in a number of ways depending upon circumstance and the activity being observed. The existence of a galaxy might be short compared to that of the Universe. The life span of a star and its planets may be short compared to the galaxy. The span of organic life in a star's environmental sphere is short when seen against the star's existence. The lifetime of an individual organic form, regardless of complexity, is short when viewed against the total evolution of organic forms.

We have chosen to measure time based on the rotation of our world and its passage in orbit around our particular star. We have divided time into convenient segments to measure change in terms of seconds, minutes, hours, days, years and so on. We talk of cyclical time, of the possibilities of time loops, of mobius-like potential, of the effects on time of material events such as black holes, and of relativity of time based on speed and perception. Ultimately however, we tend to think of time as linear, as a continuous line stretching from somewhere in the "past" to somewhere in the "future". Perhaps though, time is more like a series of dots on a piece of paper, each with its own distinct energy signature. They appear linear in nature because of a constant measurable change in the balance of energy resulting from the interaction between the actors of dispersion and evolution.

But regardless of how we measure it, time is an illusion. It is finite since it has a beginning. It is, in our perception, infinite in that we know of no ending. It is variable, within the space-time environment, being influenced by forces we are still trying to understand. It is relative, composed of subjective measurement of change as viewed from a particular viewpoint.

The change in the energy balance gives time its dimensions and substance. Yet because time exists within the Void, every instant of time, from the perspective of someone present in the Void, occurs simultaneously. Thus, from the perspective of eternity *all* things occur at the same "time" for time is itself a construct alien to the changelessness of the Void.

Evolution

The Universe derives from the spark of initial origin energy, that Light which appeared in the Void. However, it is not synonymous with it. It might be more understandable to say that the energy, and, in the case of the third view of creation, the consciousness of the Light became subsumed into the Universe at the instant of the "Big Bang"/creation. In that third view, each particle of matter, each pulse of energy, each bit of life is imbued with a fragment of the consciousness thus arrested from expansion into the Void.

In all three views of creation, within the space-time environment, evolution "fights" against entropy and diffusion by the concentration of particles of matter into complex forms within an ordered universe. However, in the second and third views, that concentration into more complex forms also includes the metaphysical essence brought into being or already contained within each particle. As such, the Universe is a distinct structure evolving according to physical and metaphysical laws. In these two views, it could be said that the material Universe is a finite tool through which the infinite is obtained.

In the first view of creation, Humanity is just the random result of material evolution governed in turn by physical law and the nature of the universe. Thus, all we are, what everything is, is just a collection of atoms, molecules, and organics governed by physical, chemical, and biological processes. Self-awareness, if it truly exists, is just an illusion, a byproduct of biological processes which exists only as long as the undamaged brain functions properly.

Self-awareness can be altered, increased, or diminished by the manipulation of those biological processes. When the organic form enabling that awareness ceases or the brain is damaged beyond repair that self-awareness disappears with no lingering presence, no soul to continue on after the mortal form has failed. As with all things, when the human physical form fails, the law of conservation of energy dictates that the energy present in the human body is simply conserved and reused within the confines of the space-time environment. We are born. We live. We die. And that is the sum of it. There is nothing else. There never was. Once you end, that's it, finito. Nothing comes after.

As such, we need not explore the first view further. There are text books and learned scientific tomes to guide one through the intricacies of physics, chemistry, and biology. We need not duplicate those works. The first view of existence is in some respects a dead end. Regardless of the complexities contained in the universe, what you see is what you get. Expect nothing more.

Views two and three begin with what is understood within the first view but embrace a broader vision of existence. It is this vision, and the attendant ramification that something beyond our physical selves exists, that lies at the heart of Humanity's attempt to make sense of existence.

In views two and three, Humanity is one result of a combination of physical and metaphysical evolution. And in view three, Humanity shares in the substance and consciousness that stems from the Light and the first moment of creation. Each individual, from the moment of conception, contains within themselves a portion of that Light, a concentrated portion of that consciousness, and is one with the Light and all else within the physical/metaphysical creation.

In both views two and three, physical and metaphysical evolution has reached a tipping point in Humanity. The combination of organic life with self-awareness and metaphysical essence no longer need be subject to inevitable entropy and diffusion. The organic body is the vessel, the temple of life that permits the conjoining, the concentration of essence, of consciousness. But it is a fragile vessel subject to the demands of mortal existence. No one, whether in pursuit of material gain or metaphysical understanding, can be certain of the "time" available in this form.

The space-time environment, with its physical universe, provides the means for evolution, enabling the concentration of the scattered elemental consciousness into organic creatures. This in turn provides the framework for the eventual evolution of a continuing metaphysical entity capable of surviving the end of the organic structure that engendered it.

Metaphysical Evolution

In creation views two and three, the space-time environment is essential to the conjoined processes of material and metaphysical evolution.

In view two, the material universe provides the nursery for the emergence of organic forms. As the complexity of organic forms increases, there arrives a point where conditions allow for consciousness and metaphysical development. Thus, it is only with the emergence of organic life that the conditions for metaphysical evolution are put in place. In this view, it is the concentration of organic matter into more and more complex structures that somehow begins a metaphysical process that culminates in a conscious entity capable of continuing beyond its organic form.

In view three, fragments of a greater consciousness are already present at the moment of creation. At each step, "in time", of material and then organic evolution, there is a concentration of metaphysical essence, that speck of consciousness each particle of matter is imbued with. This metaphysical essence undergoes a similar evolutionary process as its density and complexity increases along with increases in the density and complexity of inorganic and organic matter.

At some point, the metaphysical form, the consciousness, the spirit if you will, achieves enough complexity that it is capable of continuing beyond the end of its material framework. Where that point is, is not discernable with the tools available to us. View three allows for the possibility that a planet, a sun, or other complex solar object might be materially complex enough to achieve continuity of its metaphysical consciousness. Within this context, it is possible that these and other material objects are "alive" in a way that we do not currently understand, focused as we are in our organic-centric view of things. These "solar entities", for lack of a better term, would be incredibly long lived from our viewpoint, while we would be to them as gnats are to us in terms of comparative physical existence. However, all this changes once the metaphysical form "escapes" or transcends its material form.

In both views two and three, having reached sufficient density and complexity to survive the ending of its material form, the metaphysical entity is no longer bound to the space-time constraints of the physical universe. It exists independently from it but coexists with it and the Void within which the universe is contained. Finding itself within the Void, the entity's view of time becomes distinctly different. All of time, all material existence appears to exist simultaneously as if each of those moments were laid out before it. At this point, the construct of reincarnation, the taking of another suitable material form, becomes possible.

Most views of reincarnation envision it as moving forward from a specific point in "time" occurring at some point in the "future". However, this thought process is again a product of our linear view of time. Freed from space-time considerations, the entity would see all moments in "time" as simultaneous and thus could return to the physical universe anywhere along the space-time continuum.

Paradox and the Growing God

The ability to view all of time simultaneously raises an interesting paradox or series of paradoxes. If all time exists simultaneously from the viewpoint of the entity in the Void, then all things, all events have already occurred.

Thus all is predetermined and therefore unchangeable in the pattern of existence. However, from inside time, all things are possible, free will exists, and nothing is predetermined. Our every decision changes us and the possible futures resulting from each step, each act taken in the fullness of "life". Since the entity is free to choose where to "reenter" the universe in space-time, it may choose to "relive" the same life making different choices that subtly or significantly alter the experiences and consequences of that life on events within the timeline.

Perhaps the Everett Theory of quantum interaction may help in understanding this seeming paradox. The theory postulates that every event exists as a wave function which contains every possible outcome of the event. Instead of cumulating in a single outcome however, each of those possible outcomes is seen as being a causative branch into a new derivative timeline. Thus, multiple different and distinct timelines emerge from a single event.

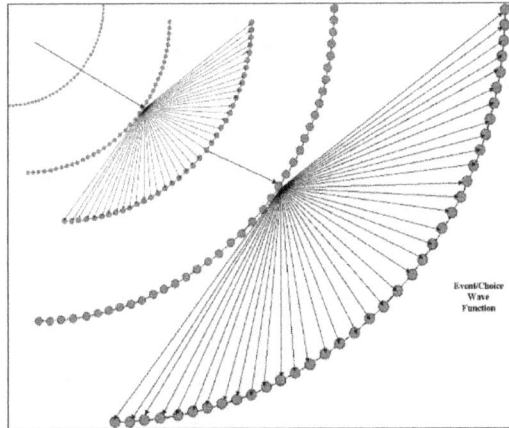

Event/Choice
Wave
Function

In this context, each new choice made by the entity in reliving the same life would not erase the previous life(s) or timeline(s) but rather create a new, parallel one. Many folks have had déjà vu, experiencing a moment as though they've lived it before. In line with the Everett Theory, perhaps this may be more than a precognitive sense of the coming moment. Instead it could be a memory of that moment as lived before, marking a point in time where a choice either has or can alter the path ahead, thus shifting that life to a new course, subtly or significantly different than previous incarnations. The ending of those déjà vu moments might coincide with the movement onto the new path, the new life yet to be explored. The entity has countless opportunities to alter the previous life path, impacting themselves and others in ways great and small. The possibilities are endless with each diverging act creating a pattern of parallel but differing existences. This has the effect of filling the Void with an expanding network of simultaneous lifetimes within the space-time environment.

This then presents still another paradox. Each layer of complexity laid down within the Void forges new pathways with each life lived and relived, with each parallel existence explored, and each choice altered in a thousand different ways. And the paradox? It is simply this. Each choice, each moment, each life is new and unique, creating new parallel and diverging pathways within the context of the expanding space-time environment. However, from the view within the Void, they have all always existed even as they are created from within the realms of time and matter.

This paradox also presents us with the construct of the growing God as the metaphysical entity explores the pathways of time and material existence, continuing to grow in metaphysical complexity. In doing so, the entity evolves in understanding and their very being to a point where the collective knowledge, the sum of experiences, the growing and ever-present permanency of existence across each parallel universe and accompanying multiverses defeats entropy and achieves ultimate survival and complete sentience.

In view two, this growing God is a result of the physical and then metaphysical evolutionary processes at work within the confines of the space-time environment. Thus, as a whole, we evolve to become God.

In view three, the God entity was present at the instant of creation with all, or at least a portion, of that entity being subsumed into that creation. It is that essence, present in each bit of the resulting material universe, which increases in complexity through metaphysical evolution. At some point, the emerging continuing entity becomes the growing God, or merges with the remnant, combining all experiences and existences as the meta-universe itself increases in size and complexity.

Multiverse and meta-universe

Since I've introduced the terms multiverse and meta-universe, let's take a moment to consider what each is. The multiverse is frequently used to include everything that exists or could exist. I use the other commonly used term "meta-universe" for that meaning. I use "multiverse" to describe a set of universes that are separated from "normal" space-time universes by a difference in the "type" of energy present in each. For my purposes, all of space-time and all possible parallel universes and multiverses are considered to comprise the meta-universe.

We've looked at how each choice within each lifetime creates a new pathway, a new space-time universe different from each of the others in some fashion. Yet each of these can be understood to exist within the same layer of energy, a "vibrational" level (for lack of a better word) if you will.

To visualize this, think of yourself as a central point with each parallel universe stretching out left and right from you across the space-time environment. In the same manner, the multiverses extend up and down from your position, separated by different "vibrations" of energy.

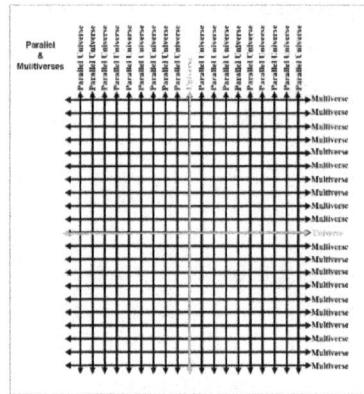

The physical characteristics, the "laws", which govern each of the multiverses may be increasingly different the further they diverge from your "central" point in space-time. The physical beings inhabiting these multiverses may likewise grow increasingly different the "higher" or "lower" you go from your "central" location as the nature of "physical" existence itself changes to suit the different contexts of the multiverses. Life in multiverses with significantly different "laws" might not be recognizable to us as such.

Religions and folk tales contain stories of beings "summoned" from another plane of existence which take on physical form, or seize the body of an unfortunate, once successfully brought into this world. Perhaps such events, indeed the very thought of gods and demons, may in some ways be nothing more than physical manifestations of multiverse beings that have managed to move or perhaps be brought to our "energy" plane of existence.

The meta-universe can be thought of as infinitely expanding as new universes and multiverses are created. Throughout, the importance of choice as a causative factor remains constant. As a continuing metaphysical entity relives a life in a physical universe or multiverse, it can and will make different choices as it explores all possibilities.

We can see these choices as the source of singularities, spawning new universes and multiverses that differ subtly or significantly from the "original". Turn left instead of right; a new universe. Say yes instead of no; a new universe. Stay in bed until 9:15 instead of 9:14; a new universe. The spider eats the fly on the left instead of the one on the right; a new universe.

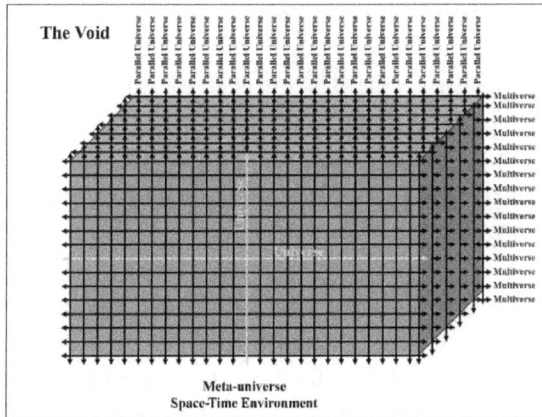

The Void
Parallel Universe
Multiverse
Universe
Meta-universe
Space-Time Environment

Choice, or perhaps even chance, if individual events are governed in a Monte Carlo sort of way, creates the fabric of space-time from which these new universes are birthed. The rock bounces straight up instead of crushing the patch of flowers; a new universe. Each choice, each chance event can occur differently, can perhaps be made to occur differently as a life is relived. These choices, these chances may appear infinite, but within the context of each "life" they may be ultimately finite as the consequences of each "second", each moment within a life are explored. Only by continuous evolution of the physical and metaphysical within each universe and multiverse can the opportunity for further growth, for eventual survival, be assured.

Evolution occurs within the context of the "physical" nature of each plane of existence. Just as each parallel

25

universe has an accompanying series of multiverses, each multiverse has its own accompanying parallel universes (multiverses). Within each, the nature of metaphysical evolution remains even as the distinction between physical and metaphysical existence may blur within "higher" or "lower" levels of multiverse existence. Thus, an emerging continuing entity finding itself in the timeless, non-spatial Void may reenter the space-time environment at any point, in any "life", in any of the parallel universes and multiverses generated by choices made while "living" in them.

In creation views two and three, our understanding of existence must expand beyond our limited view of this moment, in this place, on this world, in this universe, within an organic-centric, space-time environment. It must enlarge to include all things, all lives, all life within both the physical and metaphysical realms of existence across all material universes and multiverses.

Gods and demons, angels and devils, spirits and elementals are perhaps manifestations of life within these realms, but no less benign or deadly for being other than we think them to be. In all ways, all things are but reflections of that initial instant of existence, that initial manifestation of origin energy/Light which contained within it the seed for all things.

We are all one, across all time, across all the universes and multiverses, across all lives, across all incarnations, in whatever form or shape or energy structure we may find ourselves in, this time, this moment, within the limitless reaches of the Void. We are survival at its most essential. We are transcendence made flesh. Immortality made mortal. Timelessness captured whole within the boundaries of time. We are

- for all our flaws,
- for all our lack of understanding,
- for all our short sightedness,
- for all our insistence on this world, this life, this combination of the physical and the metaphysical as being the one blessed by God,
- for all our belief that we are the center of all that is and the foundation for all yet to be,

but one small part of the greater scheme, one small portion of the greater pattern, one small element of the infinite net of existence growing to fill the Void.

Each is unique. Each is critical. Each is instrumental to the vibrancy of the greater whole. Each is One across the span of existence. Each is linked to and composed of that elemental essence, that spark that illuminated the Void and rushes even now to fill it with infinite diversity. We are all manifestations of that beginning and of evolution in the face of entropy and destruction.

For some, the fact that we exist is the clearest indication that the Light from which we emerged has indeed survived. To them, we are finite children of the infinite within the expanding space-time environment. Each shares in the promise of eternal diversity in life as we move between the Void and the heres and nows of each existence. We are matter. We are metaphysical essence. We are energy bound together in a limitless number of ways. We are Light.

Another Round

He'd seen better days, that much was clear as he stumbled into the shade of the bar. His clothes were well worn, rumpled and unkempt, and from the smell, he'd been living in them for quite awhile. Still there was nothing shy about him as he settled slowly onto the stool next to me. He leaned his head onto his hands, rubbing his face as though gathering his thoughts. He looked hard at me, rubbed his chin with his left hand and finally spoke.

"For a taste of that, I'll tell you the meaning of life."

From the looks of him, he didn't know the meaning of water never mind the meaning of life. But I had time and had always been a sucker for hard cases, so I simply nodded and said, "Sure."

He paused for a second as though that wasn't the answer he'd expected, then he smiled and reached across to take my glass. Cradling it in both hands, he held it to his brow and moved it slowly back and forth, feeling the coldness against his sun burnt skin. After a moment more, he drank some and a look of quiet bliss transformed his face. He sat quietly, savoring each drop, until he could see the ceiling through the bottom of the glass. Then setting it softly on the bar with a wistful, reverent look, he began to speak.

"We were put here to learn. Each life the lesson's something different, but the learning's the same. ... It's a question of metaphysics."

I was frankly surprised. I hadn't known what to expect but it wasn't this. Intrigued despite myself, I nodded for him to go on. He did.

"There are three types of time: Eternity, which is endless and without change; Universal time, which is marked from the first instant of creation to the destruction of the last atom; and human time, measured from a person's birth to their death."

He paused, looking to see if I was following him. I nodded again, and he continued.

"It's a matter of evolution within those three types of time. All matter, down to the tiniest speck contains a bit of cosmic consciousness. Matter evolved from atoms to molecules, molecules to gas and dust, and then to rocks and stars and planets, and finally to organic life... ever upward, always more complex, until it resulted in sentient, self-aware creatures."

He paused again, running his left hand through hair, coarse and unkempt. With his right, he searched through his pocket 'til he came up with a stub of a smoke. He considered it for a moment before asking.

"Got a light?"

I shook my head, "Don't smoke."

He stared at the stub with a wistful expression.

"Just as well." he sighed. "These things will kill yuh."

He moved to throw it away, reconsidered in mid motion, and tucked the stub away again.

"Where was I?"

"Sentient, self-aware creatures..."

"Oh yeah." He paused again, collecting his thoughts, then continued.

"At the same time that this physical evolution occurs, there's a metaphysical counterpart happening."

"Metaphysical?"

"Metaphysical." He looked at me in quiet anticipation as though that one word explained it all.

"Go on." I said, not at all sure where this was headed. A look of resignation crossed his face and he continued as though teaching a child.

"Well, it's like this. Every bit of matter, down to the tiniest speck of dust, the simplest molecule or atom has a spiritual, an essence component to it. You see?"

Not sure I did, I nodded. Reassured, he went on.

"Just as matter evolved upward on the physical plane, metaphysical evolution occurred at the same time, matching complexity with complexity, moving ever upward until at some point self-awareness was reached and a continuing entity came into being."

"Continuing entity?"

"Right." he nodded. "A metaphysical being capable of surviving the ending of the physical existence of the frame within which it became self-aware."

I looked at him, stunned that such a philosophy would emerge from this wreck of a man. But now I was hooked, had to know where this was heading.

"So, if this entity continued beyond its physical existence, what happened to it?"

He smiled, apparently genuinely enjoying himself.

"Oh, it's still around. It passed into eternity."

"Eternity?"

"Yup. Remember when I said there are three types of time?"

I nodded slowly.

"Well the physical state exists in two of them... universal and human. The metaphysical being transcends both of those and can exist in all three."

"Including eternity?"

"Including eternity."

I scratched my head, following this but...

"So the entity passes out of the physical state of time into eternity."

"Yep."

"So, what happens then?"

It didn't seem possible, but he smiled even more broadly than before, like an angler with a fish on the line. He leaned forward with a conspiratorial air.

"You remember that universal and human time are contained inside eternity?"

"A huh."

"Well from eternity, it can survey all of time."

"So?"

"So, seeing all of existence stretched out before it, it can choose where to step back in. Choose where and how to be born. Where and how to live."

"Ah... OK. Let's say that's true. Why would it do that?"

He leaned forward expectantly. "To learn."

"To learn?"

"To learn. ... Remember I told you that was the meaning of life... to learn from each lifetime... to glean something different each time."

I sat back some on the stool seeing the circular nature of his thoughts. "So this is not your first time?"

"Nope."

"So what have you learned this time?"

He frowned a little, as though I had disappointed him.

"That the sun is hot, the earth is cold, and the milk of human kindness dries up after 6 PM."

He sat there quietly for awhile looking at me. Finally he sighed as though in exasperation.

"You just don't get it do you?"

Taken aback I replied. "Three types of time. Matter and essence. Physical and metaphysical evolution. Self-aware continuing entity passing to and from eternity to learn. Right?"

"Right."

He waited. Now it was my turn to sigh.

"Alright, what don't I get?"

He leaned forward once more, elbows on the bar, and peered sideways at me.

"There's only one entity."

"One entity... Wait..."

He waited while it slowly sunk in. "That means..."

"That's right. Only one, moving in and out of time at will... learning. Every time it's something, someone else. In fact, every person who has ever lived, is living now, or will ever live is the same being, the same person, the same entity."

"But that would mean that man's inhumanity to man..."

"Is to himself, as individuals, as a race, as a species."

I just sat there, immersed in thought, considering the implications until I finally understood.

"So you and I…"

He nodded, "Are the same person."

"Huh." I looked around the room at the few people there at that hour.

"And they're…"

"Each the same. Each you. Each me."

"Ah…"

He smiled again, clearly enjoying my confused enlightenment.

"Thirsty work that."

He held up the empty glass inquiringly. "How 'bout treating yourself to another drink?"

I laughed, neatly trapped, and ordered another round.

Reality

Reality is what you make it. That's a soft, feel-good kind of saying but, at its root, true. No two people perceive things exactly the same. You do not see the same color blue as I do. The bird may fly, but you see only the trail of the wolf in the snow.

Reality is made up of a thousand perceptions filtered through our preconceptions and beliefs. Still, there are "facts" we all agree on. We are born. We live a life surrounded by a changing world. Our existence in this mortal form ends. All else is subject to question, perception, belief, and doubt.

We hunger. We need to eat. Ah... but how much... and what should this food consist of? Food for the spirit? Food for the body? Shelter? A rock, a cave, a house of sticks, or straw, or bricks? Need versus want. Thought versus physicality. Perception versus reality.

Religion provides a framework for people, a view of the world, the universe, and all of existence. It is a panacea, a salve for wounds to the body and the spirit. It provides reason and rationality where there is none and gives comfort to the hard pressed, the weary, and the downtrodden. It gives certainty to the righteous, the true believers, and the messiahs.

Religion teaches and restricts, enlightens and condemns, saves and damns. And ultimately, religion is irrelevant to what preceded this existence and what follows it.

Religion is only important to the living for the dead have none. It shapes this existence if we let it, with strictures, laws, and commandments. It binds us to obedience, to God as represented by the Church, (pick one), its teachings, and ultimately to its leaders. It seeks moral, spiritual, and often secular control of our lives and offers the comfort of surrender, the logic of order, and the peace of having decisions concerning faith and life made for us.

Religion can be beneficial but is as often harmful and a cloak for the hidden ambitions of those who recognize its potency and its hold on the individual and the masses. It is a sham, and it blinds us. It is illusion, and yet accepted as fact. It casts only shadows while supposedly seeking light. It preys and depends on faith to sustain it, ties its faithful to it, and proclaims itself as key to salvation. It has meaning as a moral compass and a place in spiritual development. However, it is often corrupted by those who use religion's hold on the faithful in attempts at supremacy, at efforts at conquest, or in subversion of the "truth" that the religion is based on.

No matter the religion, no matter the belief, no matter the structure or the nature of the organization, all religion is created by man. It is made to fill a need: to address the basic questions that are beyond simple understanding; to justify actions that are unjustifiable except for accomplishing a greater good; to eliminate evil (which the faithful are not); and to provide order to the world and existence.

The "truth" is lost in this. That truth may appear relative or rigid depending on circumstances of birth, religion, and culture. But within a framework of metaphysical evolution, the truth is:
- that this is not the end or the beginning but part of a greater whole
- that each individual life is precious for both its potential and the actuality it represents

- that no one is more or less important than any other regardless of station, or birth, or accomplishment
- that what is done to one is literally done to all
- that all are children of the Light
- that all are one

Each life is a junction from which all else flows in infinite possibilities. Each life is a bump against the void, a mark against entropy, a step towards survival. Religion for all its claims on hearts and minds cannot change that. And yet with all its flaws and abuse of its power, religion has been as essential to Humanity as the air these bodies breath as we struggle to understand, to remember who and what we are.

People, in general, do not want to know the truth of things. We want to be comfortable. We want to have order in our lives. We want stability and the peace that comes with surrendering some part of this existence to a greater power, to *know*, that no matter what happens, it is part of some greater plan over which we have no control.

Religion gives us this. So we continue to embrace it with all its self-imposed, limited ability to illuminate or to guide the faithful to true understanding. However, the truth lies beyond the boundaries of any one religion. The totality of existence cannot be embodied in any one form or group of forms within the physical or metaphysical domains. Likewise, it cannot be captured in any one body of doctrine or religious law or teachings.

No religion is the one true faith. No religion has a monopoly on *the truth*. The mere act of capturing truth in thoughts, words, rites, rituals, and laws renders understanding moot and makes it subject to our whims, desires, needs, and failings. The search for *the truth* is transformed into a search for *our truth*, one that is acceptable within the confines of our existence.

To survive, religions seek to keep those who are born into the faith and to gain new converts. Some religions kill those who decide to leave, presenting incentive for the majority to stay. Most will stay in any event of their own accord for their religion is a part of their culture. It helps shape their lives, their thoughts, and their existence. It provides a sense of self and a sense of belonging that we as a people, as a species need, indeed cling to for reassurance and sense of importance.

A religion which encourages followers to grow beyond its confines is a religion that will cease to be. But ultimately, the aim, the goal of any religion should be:

- to provide a moral compass while freeing folk from dogma and manmade rules and restrictions
- to help folk see existence as it is without cultural or human restrictions
- to help us transcend our humanity in our understanding and in our way of living
- to show its followers the way to a greater truth

No single reason for accepting a religion, in part or in whole, applies universally. Some do it because it suits them. They embrace the teachings of a religion, its guidance, and world view. Its beliefs and tenets provide them with a foundation, purpose, and structure for their lives. Others see selflessness and sacrifice for the benefit of others and join to serve Humanity and improve the common good. Still others embrace a religion in a search for personal power and opportunities for advancement. Many might join because it is expected or because they have nowhere else to turn. But regardless of their reasons, few will admit the shallowness of teachings or the lack of understanding. To do so would create a crisis of faith and a questioning of everything they have come to depend on.

It is with honesty with oneself that understanding begins.

It is with understanding that learning begins.

It is with learning that growth begins.

It is with growth that we can achieve our true selves.

Existence is not a quirk. It is not the result of random chance although the forms we share may be the result of physical evolution. Just as the human form is not the only means to achieve sentience, neither is it the only way to achieve a continuing metaphysical entity. All things share equally in the endowment of origin essence and thus in the opportunity to achieve a gathering of spirit, the metaphysical continuing essence we call a soul. It is not unique to us, although we are vain enough and human centric enough to think so.

Reality is more than what we see. It is more than this world, with the constant sparring for control, for power, and the selfish achievement of personal ambition. Most of those who read these words will disregard them. These words are too disquieting. They do not fit with well-established worldviews. They force folk to see themselves and others differently, perhaps to live their lives differently, to accept all as equal, to see that no one, no person, no faith, no religion has all the answers.

Without the illusion that religion provides, all actions, all things, are revealed as they truly are. Everything comes from the Light. All are one with it. Because of that, ultimately every decision, every choice, every act ever done to another is done to our self. If we truly understand that, then we must live differently.

Understanding the true nature of our existence offers the opportunity for change of a fundamental nature. It holds the promise of reshaping the world by altering the way we deal with each other. However, the prospect of such change is truly terrifying, not only to those who use religion for their own purposes but also to those who cling to it for stability, for meaning, and for justification.

There is no one true faith. There is only the Light connecting us in ways obvious and subtle throughout this and every aspect of reality.

A Conversation

Two men sit in comfy chairs in front of a fireplace.

"I thought it would be different this time."

"What?"

"I said I thought it would be different this time."

"What would make you think that?"

"Oh, I don't know. (*Shrugs*) I guess I thought that after all this time, all the changes that have happened since I was last here, that people would be more compassionate, more forgiving in regard to one another."

"That is just incredibly naïve."

"I guess. But I can't help hoping that somehow people will have stopped putting a premium on material things and personal power and will just enjoy life for the beauty and joy that each brief span offers."

"Still idealistic I see."

"Well yes. I suppose I just have a broader view of things."

"So do I, but I don't share your rosy view of people, either as individuals or in general."

"If they could only remember…"

"But they can't, and I for one think that was one of the wiser decisions. No memories, no grudges, no long-term agendas. Who's to say that they wouldn't just try to perpetuate whatever world order the lucky ones on top established. Then you'd end up with perpetual servitude of the masses with full knowledge that they could never expect anything better."

"A perpetual caste system."

"Exactly. And the haves would have an eternal vested interest in keeping it that way. At least now everyone has a chance to be top dog once in a while."

"I've never agreed with that. I've always believed that if they knew, really knew the nature of their existence that they would all get along. Eternity of chance equals eternal opportunity to cooperate, to build upon the past in a meaningful way that eliminates strife, and warfare, and religious and ethnic bigotry. No more zealots. No more religious fanatics. No more hatred. Only eternal opportunities for peace, harmony, and cooperative accomplishment in an environment that recognizes love as paramount, respect as mutual, and equality as a daily fact of life."

"Naïve. Hopelessly naïve. Why do you think we fell?"

"You fell because you disobeyed. You rebelled against everything that is, that should be in the universe, in existence."

"Wrong!"

"Wrong?"

"Wrong. Look, we've been having versions of this conversation for a very long time now, but you still fail to grasp the essence of what really went down."

"I disagree. After all, I was there. I saw it all even if I wasn't directly involved in sending you here."

"Yeah. I saw you standing at the right hand and all that. But even with all that access, you still fail to understand."

"Again, I disagree, but I'm game. Explain it to me. Why did you fall?"

"You really want to know?"

"Yes."

"You're sure?"

"I'm sure."

"Positive?"

"Positive."

"Well alright then. Here it comes. It's so simple even a newt would comprehend."

"Insults aside, tell me already. Get on with it…"

"We fell… You're sure you want to hear this?"

"Oh for God's sake!"

"Just checking. We fell because we wanted to be in charge."

"In charge?"

"Yep. In charge. You see we do remember. We know, we understand the nature of existence and we wanted to be the ones on top. Wanted to shape existence in our images… to run things. Be the top dogs, the chief enchiladas, the…"

"OK, OK, I get it. You wanted to be the bosses. … That will *never* happen."

"Well DUH! … Otherwise we wouldn't keep having this conversation."

"Glad you realize that. In order for you to be in charge, you would have had to start completely over. Since everything has its basis in God's essence, you would have had to destroy everything that ever was, is, or could be… including yourself before you could do what you wanted to do."

"Matter of opinion that. I think we could have managed as things are. Just replaced the folks at the top with new management so to speak."

"Even after all this time, I think you're still deluding yourself about the real essence of existence. You could never have done what you wanted without… you know. But I am curious. What would you have done differently if you had been on top?"

"Maybe nothing. Maybe everything. We're really not that different after all… all cast from the same mold so to speak. The point here is that we would have been in charge. We have that knowledge you keep talking about giving Humanity. We know, really know what gives in the eternal world of existence. One order, unchanging. One set of instructions carried out in unending fashion across all times, all places, all lives. Good, bad, indifferent, it is what it is. There's no chance to move up, no room for ambition, no room for change. Maddening for any thinking being. In many ways, I really prefer it here among the blind, deaf, and dumb. At least they don't know and thus can grow, can change, can experience the newness that each life brings, and rise and fall without permanent consequences."

"You sound like you envy them."

"I do in a way. Don't get me wrong. I wouldn't want to be them. I *like* knowing, but I do envy the opportunities that not knowing gives them."

"How refreshing. Truth at last."

"I've always told the truth. It just isn't your truth."

"Hmmm. Well let's just say we'll agree to disagree on that one."

"If you say so… So, what brings you here this time?"

"Vacation. Won the lottery and built a sweet little getaway in the mountains."

"You didn't cheat, did you?"

"Me? Never! I just seem to be lucky somehow."

"I'm sure…"

"Since I was out this way, I thought I'd drop by."

"Glad you did. Haven't seen many of the old gang lately. They're all off building their earthly empires, being in charge you know."

"Choice as punishment."

"If you will. … Going to start a new religion this time?"

"Religion? Oh no… I've sworn off that. As a matter of fact… that religion thing wasn't really what I had in mind that time. I was just trying to teach them. To get them to understand that they had a choice, that they could love without expectations and live without fear."

"And they killed you for it. …"

"Well yes they did, but if they understood…"

(*Laughs*) "Always the optimist. So, no religion then?"

"No. Frankly I just hate what they've done with it. Twisting knowledge and spiritual teaching into a tool for personal power. Any religion that requires a police force to enforce it, to keep its followers "pure" just doesn't seem much like religion to me. It holds people back rather than…"

"Help them see the light?"

(*Laughs*) "Exactly. Anyway, no religion for me."

"Refreshingly candid. Not bad. Not bad at all."

"Thank you, I think."

"Stay for dinner?"

"I'd love to, but I think not. Maybe next time?"

"Yes. Next time. Well, give my best to your father. It really wasn't anything personal. I think the world of him. (*Laughs*) You know what I mean."

(*Nods*) "I do. He still thinks fondly of you as well. To tell the truth, I think he always had a soft spot for you. Brightest and best and all that."

"Yes well, somewhat of a disappointment I would expect."

"No. Not at all. Well, he's not exactly happy with the rebellion and all but he respects your choice, really, that you took a stand, tried to shake things up. Better yourself. In some ways I think your fight with him was responsible for the no long-term memory decision. While there, they remember everything in between and get to choose if and when to return. But nothing while here."

"Well at least it resulted in some good."

"Matter of opinion there. (*Smiles*) Funny thing though."

"What?"

"Without the knowledge of what went before, without memory, they still are aware that something more than this exists."

"You can't expect to block all memory. There's bound to be some leakage. Some insight into the great beyond. After all, we're here and we know. Some of that connection is bound to bleed over from time to time."

"Now you wouldn't have anything to do with that, would you?"

(*Smiles broadly*) "Maybe. Maybe not. Seriously though, I just think some of it just bleeds though. Can't really wall off one part of existence forever you know."

"Well it's not permanent..."

"I know... only 'til the end of times. Pretty short when you consider everything. Seems long enough while you're here though."

"I can only imagine."

"Yes, well... thanks for dropping by. Sure you won't stay for dinner? I'm making pot roast. Secret recipe. Been in the family for generations."

"Tempting... but no. I promised Mary that I'd be back by five."

"Mary?"

"My daughter. I told her I'd take her to the ridgeline to watch the sunset."

"Mary... your daughter..."

"Maggie and I really like the name. It just seemed right. It's been in the family a long time."

(*Smiles dryly*) "Right."

"Well it was good seeing you. I love what you've done with the place."

"Thanks. Drop by anytime you're in the neighborhood."

"I will.

Both move towards the door.

Dad really does miss you, you know."

"Yeah well, I miss him too kid… but sometimes things just don't work out the way you would expect… or want."

"Yeah well, see you around." (*Moves through the door*)

"Yeah. See you… (*Turns as if surveying the fireplace area, expression unreadable*) … next time."

A Question of Faith

Since the first appearance of Humanity, the fundamental question of man's relationship to God and the world around him has been answered in different ways by different cultures. Religions have been founded while others have fallen as a consequence of the answers arrived at.

All religions require their members to believe, as a matter of faith, the answers and teachings provided by their religious leaders. However, Humanity questions by nature. It is inevitable then that people should come to question their religions and the answers they provide.

In the search for God and the meaning of existence, questions may be asked that have no ready or adequate answers. People then have three choices:

- to accept the inadequacy as enough
- to reject the religion and perhaps God
- to see the inadequacy and pursue understanding

Yet it is in searching for understanding that we can sometimes be hindered by the nature of religions themselves.

It is often professed that as God created all things, so also is God within all. However, this has not historically been the thrust of most religions. Each culture, each religion has seen fragments of the truth as people sought to comprehend the nature of God and fix it firmly within the context of their daily lives. Yet the image of a hammer throwing thunder God or that of an Earth Mother Goddess became seen as unreal as images more suited to Humanity's level of sophistication and material knowledge replaced them. In the western world, the arrival of the Christ came at a time of moral and spiritual cynicism. The old religions were still followed. However, in the areas ruled by or under the influence of Rome, some reached out hungrily towards this new manifestation of God's being and will.

Nevertheless, in the midst of revelation, humans caught, congealed, and mingled this manifest expression of God's will with the designs and strictures of their own cultures and the realities and requirements of power. Christ's words, physical death, and his resurrection were codified, ritualized, and utilized as a means of enforcing and expanding temporal power by use of religion.

Once adopted as the official state religion of the Roman Empire, and safely adapted to cultural limitations, Christianity became a tool to standardize and spread that culture. Religion was and is a common, unifying force. It binds folk through a common set of beliefs, establishing a common cultural heritage which distinguishes them from others.

The Christian Church continued to be a unifying force in the West after the fall of Rome. However, political maneuvering, emerging doubts, and dissatisfaction with Church practices ultimately precipitated schism and fragmentation. Even then, fragmentation was driven as much by political goals of princes as by desire to reform a church seen as more concerned with material considerations than pursuing spiritual enlightenment.

Throughout history, this process can be found wherever religions appear. All too often, religion is used for political purposes or as a tool wielded to intimidate and subjugate others because of, or through their belief in a divine being. This focuses effort not on comprehending the nature of existence but rather on using man's cultural conception of God to further material ends. This tying of God to cultural and individual goals masks the nature of existence by eliminating those aspects that are not culturally acceptable. Each religion reveals certain aspects of existence to its followers, while ignoring those not useful or understandable in the context of day to day life. Most fail to appreciate and accept truths understood by those of other faiths.

We are taught religion as part of our cultural heritage. We are in childhood inculcated into our parent's culture. It is from them that we receive our first indoctrination into accepted beliefs. Later, our formal education often includes religious training of some form along the lines acceptable to our parents. In the innocence of childhood, we believe what we are taught. It is later, for some in adolescence, for others in adulthood, that doubt begins.

Cultural religion begins to lose its appeal as questions are asked which have no answers and restrictions on lifestyles and behavior become resented and ultimately rebelled against. A search for truth begins that, for many, starts with denial of God and ends with the embracing of another cultural religion more acceptable to the individual. But even this is temporary. Doubts erased are easily replaced by others. The reasons for dissatisfaction with one cultural religion cannot easily be erased by acceptance of another.

Cultural religions hold much truth, but they are flawed by the limitations of the culture in which they arise. Religious doubt under these circumstances is not to be considered aberrant or unnatural. It is instead to be expected and accepted as a natural state of affairs that comes into being whenever someone seeks to transcend the cultural limitations they have been immersed in since birth.

However, an individual in a quest for religious revelation and truth often finds themselves rejected as a heretic by the religion they were raised in and spurned by others as a nonbeliever and infidel. This reaction is understandable from the perspective of the "faithful". However, it serves as an indictment of Humanity's lack of readiness to expand its understanding.

The fundamental question asked for those with religious doubts has never been, "Is there a God?". Rather it has always been, "If there is a God, why then cannot my religion reveal it to me?". It is this question that, when left unanswered, may lead one into religious angst from which they may not emerge. Alternatively, it may lead to a never-ending quest for religious meaning as one finds that no cultural religion in and of itself can reveal God to them.

Finding no answer to the quest in religion, it is here that the rational person says, "If my religion cannot reveal God to me, then there is no God." This logic, although wrong, points out the foundering of comprehension. The question is not whether God exists, but rather why cultural religions cannot reveal God and the nature of existence to Humanity.

Dogma, ritual, and tradition all are fundamental aspects of cultural religion, yet it is these very foundation blocks that restrict religious growth and understanding.

Dogma is the codified beliefs of a religion.

Ritual is the expression of dogma in a stylized format as an act of worship to God.

Tradition is the cultural inculcation and repetition of dogma and ritual.

Once dogmatized, ritualized, and traditionalized, religious teachings may not be questioned without rejecting one's cultural upbringing, one's religion, or, as the last resort of rational people, the existence of God.

It is unavoidable that organized religions possess dogma, ritual, and tradition. It is inherent in their very nature. It is also inevitable that religious growth and understanding be stifled and tied to cultural goals and norms as one's religious beliefs become subject to the whims of people with political as well as religious motivations.

Empire building on Earth has always been an obstacle to discovering and disseminating truth. Yet organized religions are not in and of themselves bad if their focus is on aiding each person in achieving a greater understanding of God and existence. It is when this role is subjugated or subordinated to cultural goals and drives that organized religions lose their way.

It has often been expressed that we are engaged in a struggle for survival of the fittest, that one should take care of their own needs first, and that this is as things should be. This is thought to be humanity. Religion should help one transcend their humanity. It should not be subjugated to it.

Religious growth depends upon an environment suited to it. As the seed provides the basis for later growth, so also do the cultural religions. Cultural religions provide nourishment for the early understanding of God, even as the seed holds food for the young plant. But as the shell of the seed gives way to the plant seeking light, so also must cultural religions allow their protective shells to be cast off as one seeks new light to increase their understanding.

Cultural religions are the seeds from which mature spiritual "plants" may emerge. But just as a seed whose shell will not part will kill the plant, so also may cultural religions stifle or end the growth of religious understanding among their followers.

Each religion perceives a portion of the truth and comprehends a fragment of the total picture of existence. The way to gain greater understanding is not to deny those truths revealed in other cultural religions, but rather to first firmly establish those truths revealed in one's own faith. With this as one's roots, one may then attempt to discover whatever truths have been revealed to people in other times, in other cultures. Organized religion should provide guidance to this process without hindering it, promoting spiritual growth without attempting to restrict or channelize it. But even then, one should remain aware that all religions have a built-in cultural bias that may hinder acceptance of the existence of a greater truth.

The bureaucracy of traditional organized religions, in order to expand their flocks of faithful and semi-professing followers, exhibit a tendency towards textbook religion. This teaches, in a doctrinaire fashion, basic tenets of faith without promoting deeper understanding of the spiritual reality that provides meaning. Teaching the law without fostering understanding is a self-defeating exercise, which leads to religious doubts as the questioning of the law's relevance in modern times is translated to more fundamental questions.

Religion should seek to guide the combination of life, awareness, and metaphysical development to enable understanding of the universal truths of existence. It is the search for these truths that form the foundation of religion. Yet these concepts, these truths, are often the very things that organized religions ultimately hide and sometimes ban from their adherents as the religion becomes captured by temporal, physical concerns and bound up with excessive ritual and dogma. Hierarchies, including religious ones, face the temptation of attempting to perpetuate themselves at the cost of sacrificing the very reason they came to exist.

It does not matter if one worships God in a Latin mass or in the common tongue. It does not matter if one bows to the East, kneels to pray, or touches a holy relic or ruin as a sign of respect or holy duty. It does not matter what name one calls God. What is vital is that persons of all faiths, Orthodox, Reform, or Sectarian, truly understand that all are one. All are creatures of the Light, separate and distinct in this existence, yet one with each other. The one role of religion should be to focus Humanity's attention upon this and to guide each person to a true understanding of all it implies. For it is truly said that as you do unto others so also do you do unto your self.

Another Conversation

"What fools they are!"

"But wonderful fools."

"They are completely wrong about everything."

"Are they?"

"Of course they are! They celebrate the birth of a child as though it changed everything."

"Didn't it?"

"They still have poverty, disease, hatred, greed, wars, and all the evils that they impose upon themselves."

"Yes, but they are less now."

"Only in some places, and, though diminished elsewhere, they have only reemerged in different guises, in different ways."

"Yes. But they also have love and compassion and hope and all the things that those things bring with them."

"But that child didn't bring those things with him. He didn't cause them to magically appear with his birth."

"Every child ever born brings those things with them when they enter this world. It is a miracle that is frankly under appreciated by some."

"Point taken. Although the potential you describe is lost somewhere along the way as the child grows and matures as they age."

"It never does. The potential is always there. The capacity for love, for compassion, for hope is always present, sometimes just waiting for the right circumstance to present itself."

"Even Hitler was kind to children and dogs."

"I wouldn't necessarily say it in those terms, but yes. Inside the self-imposed boundaries of an individual life, each is capable of much warmth, affection, and caring, even if they present a different face to the rest of the world."

"Fine. But we're getting off subject here. A large part of those folks believe, truly believe that that child was born on Christmas."

"Does the day really matter that much?"

"Perhaps not. But it's indicative of the blind faith of these people."

"It's not just them."

"True. But you're only making my case. All true believers are mistaken. They have no idea about the real nature of things, of what existence is all about."

"Perhaps. But faith also helps them through the difficulties they encounter while they inhabit these lives."

"But they're wrong!"

"So?"

"A large population actually believes that that child, that you were… are, the son of God."

"And aren't I?"

"Well yes, but all of them are also God's children in a way none of them understand."

"And that bothers you."

"Yes it does. It boggles my mind that they put such concentrated devotion on one *person*, one individual among millions when each of them has the same birthright, the same heritage, the same ability to understand, to reach beyond this world and touch all else that exists, everything else that matters."

"But to them all that matters is the life that they are living now."

"But that's so short sighted."

"Is it? You and I understand based on who and what we are now, in this instant, but when we are there, we are like the rest and just like them we know nothing more, have no greater knowledge of what lies beyond."

"But that's so wrong!"

"Actually it's rather comforting."

"Comforting?"

"How would you like to be living those lives knowing, *knowing* mind you, that they have to endure everything they will meet not only in the life they're in at that moment but in all the lives they may ever live and that the person inflicting pain on them is in fact themselves in another form, in another life."

"Now that I imagine would be true torture."

"Yes it would. You remember that lives lived on that plane seem to pass so slowly at times? Well imagine knowing *everything* at birth and remembering it without the blessing of forgetfulness. What if you knew that you would live to be 100, that the world as real and beautiful and terrible as it is, is a place made up to ensure one's survival, to create the very means of existence and that each life, each act, each thought, each stone and tree and blade of grass were instruments to further that end? How would you feel as you waited out your days? Would you revel in them? Would you dread them? Would you try to make them see, to understand the true nature of reality or would you let them live their lives in quiet and noisy ignorance with none the wiser for your passage?"

"You are talking of yourself here aren't you?"

"In a way. I'm torn sometimes between wanting and knowing. Wanting to tell them… me… us and knowing that, even if I did, it would do no good, that the truth would not fit with the lives they have in the moment they live them, and if I did, when I did… they would only understand a bit of what I said, what I showed them, and convert it, use it to provide meaning for who they are now, then, in each of the incarnations."

"As I said, they're fools."

"And again… No. Just amnesiacs seeking to understand the basic questions of existence."

"And failing."

"Yes. And failing. But then you and I know that what they understand is unimportant. What they do is unimportant. How they live is unimportant as long as they live, as long as they do something, as long as they exist and create the possibilities of other times, other places, other realities. But they would live differently if they understood. They would treat themselves better."

"Or not."

"Or not?"

"You know there are some who understand but pretend not to."

"Pretend not to?"

"Yes. For if they understood they *would* have to act differently, treat their fellows as themselves, love them, care for them, etc. It's just too inconvenient."

"Inconvenient?"

"They'd have to give up the power they have over others and truly try to help them… instead of seeing them and using them as instruments to enforce their personal version of God's will."

"Perhaps. But most are spared that choice, that knowledge. This way they can live these lives in oblivion, being certain in their faiths and views of things. They can celebrate births and mourn passings with the "knowledge" that a "better place" awaits, that tomorrow must be… will be better than today, and salvation is theirs if only they obey the laws, follow their religious teachings, to prevail against all evil."

"Even when that in itself is a source of the *"evil"* they see elsewhere? Even when those leaders they follow are motivated by greed and lust and ambition? Even when the religions they embrace have little to do with truth and spiritual advancement? Even when they are blinded by faith and fueled by hatred for the impure, the apostates, and the heretics? Even when unspeakable things are done in the name of righteousness and God?"

"Even then."

"What fools they are."

"Yes. But wonderful fools. For, for them all things are possible and from them all else comes."

"But they are still… fools."

Of Good and Evil

What then of evil?

What of the suffering and pain in the world? Why does it exist?

Some suffering, some pain is the unfortunate result of changes that occur in the world. The universe is governed by physical laws that provide cause and effect for events such as hurricanes and earthquakes. Even evolution itself places obstacles in our way in the nature of germs and viruses that mutate and evolve to better target our cells and other organic structures. However, in large part, Humanity is responsible for a great deal of its suffering. And as we create this suffering, it is within our ability to end it as well.

One might be tempted to say that "evil" does not exist. After all, it's really pretty much a situational us versus them kind of thing. What *they* do is "evil". What *we* do is just, good, righteous, approved and allowed by God and our view of the world. Often the actions of two opposing groups are indistinguishable. Each views its own behavior as good, as justified, as "Godly" and the behavior of the others as unjustified, as bad, as "evil". Evil is a term used to justify actions, to vilify a person, a group, or a nation/country. It is used to represent activity or a way of life that is strange, different, and/or in opposition to our own. And whether we be steeped in tribal traditions or tied to urban preconceptions, it is easier to call something evil and destroy it than to understand it.

If someone is seen as different, as "evil", there is less reason to hesitate in taking action to benefit oneself at the expense of that *other*. But what if we are all one despite the surface differences? Should we still act the same?

Some religions have put this as a choice between spiritual growth and the attainment of material wealth and power although many religious leaders often seem to confuse the two. The choice can be phrased this way. Which do I prize most highly; position, power, and influence in material and worldly things or spiritual understanding, growth, and development? The two are often cast as mutually exclusive. The truth is less clear, more nuanced, with most people seeking to achieve both, placing different emphasis upon the two "choices" at different times during their lives. Still, although the choice is not necessarily as black and white as it may seem on the surface, the two paths, material and spiritual, are not easy to reconcile and are not often found to be in harmony with one another.

Christians are taught that Christ laid out the choice in this fashion. "For what shall it profit a man, if he shall gain the whole world, and lose his own soul?"[1] or "what shall a man give in exchange for his soul?"[2] However, material gain and spiritual understanding are not necessarily incompatible. One can have material progress without forsaking spiritual growth and vice versa. One does not have to be attained at the expense of the other. However, to achieve both without the sacrifice of one or the other requires a fundamental change in Humanity's view of creation, the universe, this world, and ourselves.

It should be the vocation of religion to enable this transcendence of understanding; to prepare Humanity to understand that the choices are not exclusive; that one's own gains should not be made at the expense of the wellbeing of others (and I don't mean that you should turn

---

[1] King James Bible, Mark 8:36
[2] King James Bible, Mark 8:37

down that promotion because only one of you can have it); that all are truly one.

If this is true, if all are one, what then is the nature of evil?

Some might describe evil as the opposition of the good. It might be considered a twisting of the "rightful" way of things into patterns that are harmful to body, mind, and spirit. Perhaps more appropriately, it might be seen as the purposeful harming of others through action or inaction or as the attempt to benefit oneself or a select group of individuals through the deprivation, subjugation, or destruction of others.

There are of course subtle shades of gray in this. One might truly believe that they were acting for the good of all and as a result of well-meaning action still perpetrate terrible suffering and harm on an individual, a group, or a people. Some of this may come from one's cultural perspective, "We must bring civilization to these savages!", and sometimes results from a misplaced desire to bring the "benefits" of one's own cultural or religious views to the rest of the world. Other times, this results from a calculated design to place oneself and others above the rest, to gain, by whatever means necessary, the wealth, comforts, and privileges of this world, no matter what the cost. Still, beyond these obvious stereotypes come the blurred ones, the ones that seem good but may result in something less than the intent.

If I give a beggar money, will the beggar use it for food or for something less beneficial such as drugs? Is the act of giving the beggar money made less good, less meaningful by the beggar's decision? Or does an act of generosity, out of genuine concern for one's fellow, have an intrinsic value of its own regardless of the ultimate outcome? How far should one go to care for one's fellows? What is the extent of caring? Do we remove the element of chance? Do we remove choice? Do we prevent the possibility of harm by eliminating the opportunity for it to occur? Or is this just another harm disguised as well-meaning care for the disadvantaged?

Whether this constitutes "evil" often depends upon one's point of view. Evil is not easily described or avoided. What is a blessing for one may represent great harm and suffering, "evil" to another. Some activities, some acts, some purposes are commonly understood as bad, as harmful, as "evil". However, on a day to day basis determining "evil" across the daily activities in one's own life is seldom clear cut. It often hides within the brightest of acts and the most seemingly best of intentions.

Yet there can be no evil unless Humanity allows it to exist. Wars, starvation, slums, the countless sufferings of us all are the symptoms of the lack of understanding or the willful disregarding of the knowledge that all are one. Yet even in a perfect universe, where all work for the betterment of all, where all understand that what one does to another they do to themselves in another form, in another life, one cannot guarantee that no harm, that no suffering will occur. But working as a united whole, that suffering, that harm, that "evil" can be minimized or reduced.

Of course, this is easy to say when one is not facing starvation with inadequate food or water for all. It is easy to say when one is not faced with purposeful destruction of property, of villages, of livestock at the hands of an invading force. It is easy to say when one is not faced with someone who does not understand or who willingly sets aside that understanding to benefit themselves in the pursuit of power, wealth, and/or control.

Realizing all are one does not mean that one should not defend oneself. It does not mean that one should submit to attack or assault, robbery or rape, threats or intimidation. It does mean that one should always be mindful of the way of things when dealing with others and resist the temptation to replace the views of others with one's own through subjugation or other types of control. There is room for diversity. There is room for choice. There is room for opportunity and random chance and differing beliefs. There is even room for "evil" but one does not have to submit to it or encourage its existence.

"Evil" will continue to exist as long as one person places themselves above another. It will continue to thrive as long as one person seeks to control others for their own benefit. It will continue to flourish as long as religion is used as a tool for personal advancement, as a control over a population, or to sustain a religious bureaucracy. It will continue to be present as long as one person thinks of themselves as better than another, more suitable, more entitled, more holy, or more righteous. It will continue as long as one person believes that they come first; that their welfare is more important than that of others; that the world would be better off without its "surplus population"; that one race is superior to another; that the poor are that way because they deserve to be; that their interpretation of God is better than another's; that any human being is less important than any other. In short, Humanity needs to transcend itself, to see beyond the confines of this existence, to understand that all are truly one within the Light in fact as well as in religious or philosophical platitudes.

But what about good and evil? Why do both exist?

Regardless of how we define them, regardless of how our culture sees them in terms of specific acts, activities, thoughts, and rationales, why do they exist? The span of creation contains within it the potential for all things. However, neither good nor evil were created. They exist as a consequence of actions or inactions taken by sentient beings in the course of their existence.

The *possibility* of evil exists just as the *possibility* of good exists. Good can exist without evil just as indeed evil can exist without good. It is impossible however to define the existence of one without the presence of the other. One may be joyful but not know that to be joyful is to be desired because sorrow has never been experienced. This does not mean that both must exist for the one or the other to exist. It does mean that both must be *possible* if either is to have true meaning.

Freedom of choice permits the existence of both Good and Evil. But to even have that construct at all, one must first have creatures that are capable of choice and definition of that choice as either a good or bad thing. Without that awareness, that understanding, that cultural definition, the choice is just a choice. I hunt the rabbit instead of the pig. I drop the rock on the turtle. I burn down the village. These are just choices without some relevant cultural distinctions to "decide" whether the choice and the accompanying action or inaction is "good" or "evil".

Once that cultural definition exists, it is now possible for choices to be defined as a conscious decision to act in a way that is culturally acceptable or beyond what is viewed as proper and good. However, just because a culture views something as good or evil does not make it so. Terrible things have been done and viewed as "good" by the people who did them. Beneficial things have been viewed as "evil" and the people who did them persecuted, hunted, and killed because what they did was strange, threatening, or beyond the knowledge of the current cultural level.

The definitions of good and evil have a way of changing as a culture evolves. But as civilization itself evolves, these definitions have a way of being codified into behavioral practices and then into laws which form the social contract which binds the culture together and forms the framework within which "good" and "evil" comes to be viewed.

Within these frameworks, the moral guidelines that are established by each culture and civilization provide the background against which choices are made. "Good" is often seen as a reflection of light with "evil" being represented as moving towards darkness. This is an easy way to picture the difference between two choices. Light is representative of increased spiritual understanding and choices made for the benefit of all. Darkness is representative of those choices made for the benefit of one's self at the expense of others with focus on the here and now and little or no consideration of the spiritual consequences.

Cast in this way, existence becomes a morality play with distinct winners and losers not based on the material success obtained but rather by the compromise of principles, moral stature, and loss of spiritual development experienced by individuals, groups, peoples, and nations. Within this cultural context it is within each person to make basic choices between light and dark, between "good" and "evil". They cannot escape those choices anymore than the night can stop following the day. People may not stop and say out loud, "I have chosen.", but each will choose in their own way.

Some concepts, some beliefs about what is "good" appear throughout our cultures. One shall not kill is a common theme in "civilized" societies. Even there however there is some ambiguity about what is a justified killing and what is a wrongful killing. It seems there is no absolute. The line blurs to adjust to the needs of the society and the individuals who live within it.

Perhaps these cultural definitions are necessary for the successful operation of cultures and civilizations, indeed, even to allow people to live among one another in some semblance of harmony. However, what is lost within this construct is the understanding of *why* it is important to act in a particular way. Yes, it is wrong to murder someone. But *why* is it wrong? Is it wrong because someone was given tablets of stone from a God that inscribed them with the words forbidding it? Is it wrong because a King or a prophet enacted a series of laws in order to govern a city or a people and make them able to conduct the day to day affairs of life? Or is it wrong because that other person is *you* in reality as well as in religious platitude and to do harm to them in fact does the same harm to yourself even though you won't experience it until you wear that frame?

The Void is timeless. With metaphysical evolution, the continuing metaphysical entity may reenter the meta-universe in any universe or multiverse, at any point in time, as any person. Therefore that other person *is* you right now. You simply may not be able to believe it because of the blinders, the forgetfulness that physical existence imposes upon us all to some extent or another.

Of course, if that other you is trying to kill *this* you, it really doesn't matter whether or not it is you in another form. Your current form has as much value as the other and you should defend yourself to preserve the possibilities inherent in that current existence. But wouldn't it be "good" if everyone lived differently, if there were no *us* versus *them*, only *us* working with *us* to achieve a common good for all? It is within the ability of Humanity as individuals and as a whole to choose a "better" path. Pain and suffering caused by the *us* versus *them,* "good" versus "evil" mentality can be stopped. "Evil" cannot exist without our acquiescence. We can choose a better way.

Old Wisdom
A Fable

Once, not so very long ago, a young boy sat with his grandfather under the shade of an apple tree. Young boys are very curious and full of questions. This one was no different, holding a deep abiding respect for the wisdom of his grandfather. They sat there silently, enjoying the heat of the summer day, until the boy, as boys will do, sought answers from the wisdom sitting near him.

"Grandfather; What makes the North wind blow?"

"Pride." replied his grandfather.

"But what makes it stop?"

"Reason." came the response.

"What makes the flowers bloom?"

"Joy." answered the old man.

"What makes them turn brown and dry?"

"Sorrow." came the voice again.

"Grandfather; What makes the sun shine warm and bright?"

"Love."

"What then makes the nighttime come?"

"Ignorance."

"But Grandfather, if that is so, what makes the stars shine at night?"

"Knowledge."

"Then what brings the clouds that block the sky?"

"Fear."

"And the calm amidst the storm?"

"Hope."

At last emptied of questions, the boy grew silent and still, thinking on what his grandfather had told him. And there, safe in the shade, the warmth of the clear summer day gently lulled him to sleep, innocent in the shelter of his grandfather's arms.

Prelude to Understanding

Why was evolution in God's creation guided in such a way as to create Humanity? Was the evolution even guided? Why did humans emerge from the other creatures on this planet? Why does Humanity exist at all? What is its role in this world? Why is a person born to live the life they do, with the myriad choices between doing "good" or causing harm open to them? What if any role remains after shedding the metaphysical womb of a mortal body?

Questions. There always seem to be more questions. But perhaps, just perhaps there is one answer that makes sense of it all.

Evolution does not stop with the development of Humanity as self-conscious, self-knowing, mortal beings. It continues from "birth" through "death" in every lifetime. "Life" in this context serves as a developmental stage for the further evolution of the metaphysical entity that continues as the mortal frame "dies".

Like a fetus in the womb, we do not know the exact nature of existence beyond these bodies. Our awareness is limited to what surrounds us. Like the fetus, we catch glimpses of what lies ahead. We become aware of vague sounds, feelings, and sudden intuitions. These physical and spiritual innuendoes cue us that there is something more than just the limited confines of the life womb that surrounds us.

This physical existence is a learning ground which enables the metaphysical existence that follows. Take a child and put it in an adult's body and you have a large child. Take that same child and have it grow, experience, and develop through a span of decisions, actions, and inaction and you get an adult. One can take cosmic dust and return it to the spiritual essence from which it came but it shall remain unconscious. It shall remain dust. It is the evolution of this cosmic dust, with Humanity as an intermediary stage of continuing evolution, which makes it possible for the self-conscious continuing metaphysical entity to emerge.

Why should this evolution from dust to self-conscious continuing metaphysical entity exist? What is the reason for it?

 Remember the emergence of the Light/origin energy in the Void and the diffusion effect counterbalanced by the act of creation. Physical and metaphysical evolution is the consolidation of the metaphysical "consciousness" spread within the Void/eternity by appearance of the Light and the act of creation. It is the consolidation of the cosmic dust into the physical universe as we know it. It is the further consolidation of this material into organic life.

Continued consolidation through evolution into self-conscious, sentient beings establishes the conditions required for the "birth" of a metaphysical entity capable of sustaining itself beyond the confines of the material universes and multiverses. And only then do we arrive at a stage where reincarnation in all lives throughout the meta-universe occurs as the entity evolves in complexity and sentience. Thus, the growing God emerges, allowing for survival in the face of entropy and diffusion within the Void.

This is what all cultures and their associated religions glimpse and struggle to understand. But all too soon that struggle to find and understand the "truth" is subordinated to the very real concerns of daily life. In order to create order from perceived chaos and provide meaning to existence, that initial glimpse is codified, dogmatized, and ritualized to fit into the constraints of what the culture can accept. Once comfortably captured in this fashion, the "truth" is seen through a lens of cultural bias. In such circumstance, there is little or no incentive for most to pursue answers beyond what common wisdom can provide. Once squeezed to fit the culture, the "truth" is seldom pursued vigorously again.

Memory

I awoke,
not knowing who
I was or why,
what place this was
or who it was
asleep beside me
in a bed
not known as mine.

A sense of self remained,
but nothing else
to guide me
past the rocky path
to recollection.

What emptiness
to find oneself
a stranger
in a strange place.
Daunting in its barrenness,
the very walls
mock the absence
of permanent
remembrance.

Struggling past the clues
to pierce the shell
of absent knowledge,
I find a hint,
a piece of who I am
now within this place,
this life,
this bed.

And in a rush
the rest returns,
though sluggishly,
as though reluctant
to resume this life
when others have
equal call,
equal claim
upon my consciousness.

I have returned to now
and home and memory
of the self that lives
and breathes the air
of this time and place.
But still I remember
the emptiness
before the knowing.

Where was I
that I forgot
the matters
of this time,
this place,
this life?

I cannot now recall.
But knowing blankness
as a child born,
I look to pierce
the veil to gain
the essence that remained,
that questioned
in the darkness
which place this was,
that searched to find

the memory that would
mark me as myself
and secure me to this spot.

No matter.
It will come.
For now I know
the self remained
without the memories.

Unmarred by thought
of past,
of present,
of future times,
but resting still
I stay,
within this frame,
this form,
this bed,
'til memory
comes again.

Faith – Knowledge – Choice

Religion has been a keystone of our existence since Humanity first stopped to question what our place is in the cosmos. Faith in a supreme being, or beings, has been shaped and molded by the religions that emerged over time to answer that question. Yet frequently, faith in that Supreme Being, in a God, has been subordinated within churches and sects to the material concerns of power.

Often the drive for material wealth or power has crippled an otherwise vibrant and potentially strong force for enabling spiritual understanding. Even the leaders of religions can cease to be able to tell the difference between their own desires and those of the God that they profess to serve. People place their trust in these religious leaders as the holders of the keys to the kingdom. Believers accept instruction and many do as they're told. The rich and the powerful doubt everything, buy what and who they can, and conspire against those they cannot.

Within this environment, it becomes less important to know God individually as long as one knows that the religious leaders are in touch with God. People give their faith to the leaders of their churches, temples, synagogues, mosques and other places of worship and blindly follow clerics who unfortunately sometimes have no real interest in finding or understanding God or in spiritual development.

Faith is a powerful thing. Rule men's souls and their bodies will follow. Wars are gladly fought by those who believe that they are doing God's work. Unfortunately, in reality they are often only advancing the economic and/or political goals of their secular and/or religious leaders.

It has always been so, that blind faith and the search for the reality of existence have been on opposite sides of the spectrum. Blind faith keeps people chained to the whims and dictates of those who say they know. Knowledge of the nature of existence and one's relationship within it sets one free. Thus, that knowledge has often been suppressed by those who wish to gain or maintain control over institutions, people, and nations.

Knowledge brings with it true choice. It brings the ability to act, or not, with understanding of the consequences.

If you were blind, your sins would be forgiven. Since you say you see, your sins remain.[3]

---

[3] Paraphrase of John 9:41: King James Bible

The coming season

Enjoy the coming season.
It may be the last we have.

No one can see the future
except as glimmers
past the window of today.
It shifts.
It changes by the deeds done now.

We plan
but we cannot assure
that fortune
will smile on our endeavors.

We save
but we cannot say for what.

The future is as it will be.
It is beyond our grasp
and shall not be
as we envision it now.

The plate is broken.
If it is mended
can it be what it was before?

The wheel has turned.
Can we have it retrace its route
and stop
to improve the course taken?

They say
we are the sum of all we were.
I say

it is what we are that makes us us
and being creatures of choice
we can choose to be what we wish.

We can remake ourselves
in our own image
without the boundaries
and restraints
some might think would pattern us.

There is no fixed plan.
(There is
but we are not shaped by it.)
We are constrained
only by ourselves
and need not fear,
or hate,
or love
except by choice,
except by need
to rationalize our decisions.

Civilizations rise.
Civilizations fall.
It is all the same.

Religions bind.
Reason loosens the ties
but keeps the ones
most comfortable to us.

Belief is a drug.
Reason the cure
that cuts through illusions
and false justifications.

Beware the one
who knows all things,
who is omnipotent,
who casts the world
as white and black,
right and wrong,
good and evil.

That one
will take your choice from you.

That one
will have you comfortably bound
with reason left on holiday.

With belief,
one does not need to think.

Without thought
there is no reason.

Without reason,
there is no choice.

Without choice,
all futures are the same
with tomorrow
a cold and barren place.

Enjoy the coming season.
It may be the last we have.

The Sky Is Blue Today

The sky is blue today. What meaning does this observation hold? None. For the sky is blue every day even if on some the mist or fog or clouds should hide its glory.

There is no meaning there. But... how often do we notice that blueness? How often do we gaze into the endless depth of sky and search for what we cannot see, immersed in the immensity of creation, submerged beneath that endless blue?

Listen. The bird beyond the window sings its morning song. It has before. But today I listened. Today I heard the empty silence filled by notes of pureness and delight. Even so, as I listened, I heard them falter and then end as they fell upon the world unanswered even as joy exists within a world that does not see.

Exist for the moment. It is not that the past and future do not matter. They are what we were and what we shall yet be. But wait, this instant, and see and listen and exist within the essence of the moment. Be a partner in its passage and not simply passenger, asleep between the tunnels on the way, missing moments of exquisite light and scenery in the haste to end the journey.

The sky is blue today.

Doctrine

Once dogmatized, ritualized, and traditionalized, religious teachings are formed into a body of thought, rules, and laws that are called doctrine. These teachings become the foundation to perpetuate religion and to govern the behavior of true believers and adherents to the faith.

Invariably, doctrine is manmade, centering on the central tenets of the religion. It also provides definitions of sin and improper behavior, and what constitutes proper religious observance.

By definition, because doctrine is manmade by the leaders of a religion, the head of that religion is infallible in its interpretation. Note that this doesn't mean that the leader is infallible or that he or she has a direct link to God and speaks on behalf of that deity. It only means that they can change the laws any time they want because they or their predecessors wrote them in the first place.

There is no intrinsic reason why one could not leave one religion and study the tenets of another in order to increase one's knowledge and spiritual development. However, for a religious bureaucracy to allow this to occur without dispute would be at odds with the imperative of all bureaucracies to perpetuate themselves. As we noted previously, the doctrine that to leave a religion is an offense punishable by death is a major incentive for persons to remain a faithful member of that religion. Ultimately though, such a doctrinal stance has no basis in enabling spiritual development. It merely seeks to prevent those who find the religion too constricting or not illuminating enough from leaving.

Doctrine gives a religion the means to explain existence through an acceptable worldview. However, it also provides a way of ensuring obedience to a religion's leadership and of maintaining a body of followers to ensure the survival of the religion itself. After all, as in the instance of the doctrine of original sin, if everyone is born into this world with a burden of sin, that sin can only be expunged through faithful adherence to the tenets of one of the world's religions. And as a person builds up a body of sin through the course of one's life, that sin can only be removed by following the established paths to forgiveness each religion provides.

Original sin does not exist. It is a doctrine created to explain why Humanity must suffer the pain and sorrows of everyday life while showing the basic sinfulness of Humanity stemming from the original mistake made by the first humans. Coincidentally, the only way to achieve salvation, to rid oneself of Humanity's basic sinfulness, is to follow the tenets and the dictates of one of the world's religions. A man-made answer to a man-made problem.

All babies are born in innocence. They have not yet had time to learn the cultural morays and traditions that define what "good" and "evil" are. Thus all choices are the same to them. Basic knowledge is acquired first. If one cries, one will be picked up, fed, or changed depending upon the need. Ouch! That's hot or sharp or cold. I'd better not do that again! Only later, on a gradual basis, does the child learn what is "right" or "wrong" based on the reaction of its parents. One must have a framework within which to operate before choices become meaningful in the context of "good" or "bad", "right" or "wrong".

The Old Testament of the Bible is a basis for the doctrine of original sin. The story of Adam and Eve lays out their original sin of disobedience to God. Their exile from the Garden of Eden is seen as a punishment for eating the fruit of the Tree of Knowledge and a precaution to prevent them from eating from the Tree of Life. According to doctrine, each descendant of these first two humans bears the stain of that first act of disobedience and thus we are cast out into the world to make our way. The Christian rite of baptism provides an instrument to wash away that stain and make one pure once more in the sight of God.

If we take the story of Adam and Eve at face value, these ultimate ancestors were created in innocence. They lived in harmony and bliss within Eden with all of God's creation. Adam and Eve in their innocence were ignorant of right and wrong until after they ate of the apple from the Tree of Knowledge.

After they ate of that apple their eyes were opened and they saw. They gained the knowledge of right and wrong and learned what sin was. They learned that disobedience to the word of God was wrong.

Prior to the eating of the apple, they could not have sinned for they did not understand. Thus the act of eating the apple could not be a sin for they did not know it was wrong until *after* they ate it. There can be no sin without understanding, without the context of right and wrong to operate within. Thus there is no original sin to pass on. There is no need for a doctrine to provide for the washing away of sin where none exists. All children, born in innocence, must learn the cultural context of sin in order to be capable of incurring it.

Taken figuratively, the story of Adam and Eve teaches that obedience to God is of paramount importance. Of course, God can't easily be reached to provide day to day guidance and explanations. Therefore, it is vital that the people listen to and obey the dictates of God's chosen ones, the clerics and the leaders of the various religions who interpret God's will for those not fortunate enough to be in God's inner circle.

Thus, obedience to religious leaders comes to take the place of understanding and spiritual development. Blind faith becomes encouraged by those same religious leaders acting as intermediaries for God. The word of the religious leaders becomes the word of God and to disobey the leader is to disobey God. Manmade rules and laws replace the search for understanding. Religions cease to be anything other than enforcers of limited cultural beliefs and traditions and a means to achieve and maintain temporal power through the use of spiritual authority.

It is in this way that doctrines become a bulwark for the authority of religious leaders and religious bureaucracies. The teaching of these doctrines is done under the guise, often believed by those teaching them, of promoting spiritual growth though the exploration of the teachings of the religion. Successful religious teaching creates a good and faithful follower of that religion. If you do not follow the teachings of the religion, then surely you are not in God's grace. If you leave the religion then surely you have doomed yourself, if not in this life then surely in the one to come.

What impressionable young person when surrounded by the religion of their family and/or culture would not choose, at least initially, to follow what they are told is the only path to God and salvation? Organized religions place obedience to the religion above the understanding of existence and one's place within it. Because of this, most individuals are ill prepared when faced with doubts that arise as they find religious teachings are not enough to provide them the answers they crave when faced with the dilemmas of life.

Doctrine ultimately serves the religion that creates it. One must see beyond doctrine, move beyond the strictures of any organized religion to see the truth of things.

I Stand Alone

I stand alone and weep
for the loss of innocence,
for the beginning of sorrow,
for the curtailment of joy.

Had I known the price
would I have chosen less,
demanded more,
scaled the heights
to grasp at glory
fleeting though it be?

Perhaps.

Choice is a demanding thing,
depriving all excuses
from the self-made fate.

I choose.

Such finality.
Each captured moment
struck in bronze
within these words.

I choose.

And should I not
the choice is made
and still the moment
passes beyond reach
but always
in remembrance
and regret.

Regret for choices
ill-timed or ill made.

Remembrance
for the items
left undone
and those fulfilled;
for sorrow endured
and joy embraced;
for voices heard
and voices stilled,
their meanings lost
in the silence.

Yet silence is itself a choice;
to stand and watch
while others have their way,
to rest your needs
against the firmness of your mind
and find abstinence
a weak strength
and a strong weakness
in the pursuit of things.

Becalmed
within the whirlwind.

Cool
within the fire.

Still
within the frenzied
pace of life.

Choice.
Before as behind.

No less.
No more.

The way is clearly marked
as are the shadows
in the night.
One cannot tell
one from the next
except by moving
through the depths
to merge
and find oneself
as shadow
and as light
within the moment.

All things,
All thoughts,
All deeds,
engender by themselves
a debt that only
we, ourselves, can pay.
No other has the coin
for that redemption.

The price is dear
in choices made
and consequences paid
to each,
to all,
and none.

For in the midst of days
do we find ourselves alone
to shelter in the
solitude of choice,

to carry forth
the burden of our making.

Behold,
the very making of a man,
the movement
here and there
of great import
but little consequence.

Each step made
blurs in passage
to become,
as a single grain
upon the beach,
unknown
and unnoticed
in its singularity,
and yet foundation
of future lives.

In each,
choices made
and frightful coinage paid
that it be so.

And for all the choices
and the price thus paid…

I stand alone and weep.

Understanding

If you truly understand

- that whatever you do to someone else you do to yourself;
- that when someone steals, they are stealing from themselves;
- that when dealing drugs, you sell to yourself;
- that when ignoring the homeless or the beggar on the street, you ignore yourself;
- that when you hurt or abuse a child, a friend, a spouse, a parent, or a foe, you do so to yourself;

then you must live this life differently. You must be different in how you see the world and all that share it. But you must not expect others to understand, to see as you do.

Some are afraid, for those who teach the way are seen as prophets, saints, heretics, blasphemers, gods, and devils. The fate of these is seldom pleasant. And in the eyes of the world, they are often made to be more or less than they are.

Some understand but do not act, for to do so would be inconvenient to the comforts and the shelter of this life.

Some understand and willfully ignore or twist that knowledge to gain advantage over others to the benefit of themselves.

Some are blind and do not see, do not wish to see, for their faith gives them the license to behave as they wish under the guise of religion and "truth".

Some simply follow, for it is comforting to have a path to travel, to know where each step should go during this life's journey.

Each in their own way seeks the light, if only, once glimpsed, to turn away to dwell in the shadows cast in the reality each creates for themselves individually and collectively.

Yes, you must live your life differently if you understand. But you must still police, you must still defend, you must still be wary of those who do not, who choose not to see. But in doing so, you must treat them as you would yourself for they are you in different clothes, in different lives, in different existences. But they are still you. For it is a paradox of existence that even as you understand in this form, in this life, in another you may not.

The same truth is discovered, come to be understood from time to time across the centuries. But it is discarded, put aside, or converted into something more acceptable, more in line with what we see as reality. The truth is inconvenient. It doesn't fit with what we see and experience every day. It interferes with our perceptions of power and weakness, joy and sorrow, deserving and undeserving, wealthy and poor, the haves and have nots, true believers and infidels, the saved and the cast out.

If we truly understood, if we truly knew the truth, our eyes would be opened and we would see. If we truly saw then we would be responsible for our actions, each and every one of them. We would have to live our lives differently, dramatically differently, because we would truly know

- that *all of us are the same*;
- that *all of us are one*;

- that *what we do to one, we do to all, and our self.*

And that, that realization, that knowledge would be transformative. It would preclude the search for power as the aim of ambition. It would eliminate the quest for wealth as a means of personal fulfillment. It would change the view of haves and have nots, of deserving and un, of one religion being better than another and perhaps of the concept of religion itself. We would come face to face with our mortality and immortality and all else.

All worldly happenstance would be revealed as conceit, as a means to an end, as self-deception, as imaginings. This does not mean that each moment, each instant, is not important. They are. For each person, each experience across the continuum of existence is unique. Each thought, each decision, each action may occur only once for that individual in that situation in that time, regardless of how many "times" that life is lived, regardless of how many lives there are across the infinite span of existence.

Each life is precious. Each is important in and of itself. If we truly understood that then we would live our lives in profound unity, in complex simplicity, in radical harmony joined by common purpose and the realization that the good of all is more important than the benefit to some or to a single individual.

But this understanding is inconvenient. It does not match what we think we understand. It does not line up with how we want things to be. And we do not want to be responsible, truly responsible, for *all* our actions.

Prayers from a heretic

A spear of light broke the darkness as the door opened inward. Shielding eyes with an upraised hand, the sparingly dressed figure sitting on the floor could just make out the silhouette of a form standing within the doorframe. After a moment, the one on the floor spoke to the other and an exchange began as it had so many times before.

"I pray for you every day my friend."

"I am not your friend."

"Perhaps not. But I still pray for you."

"I do not need your prayers heretic. You will die now. Are you ready?"

"No one is ever ready. It is always a surprise even if expected."

"Prepare yourself for you must die."

"Why?"

"You are an affront to the faithful everywhere."

"This you must explain to me. In what way am I an affront?"

"You blaspheme the holy tenets of our faith."

"How is that possible?"

"You question our ways and the teachings of our most Revered Leader. This cannot be tolerated."

"Why not?"

"There is only one true faith. Ours. Anyone who believes otherwise must be… shown the error of their ways."

"How?"

"They must be punished for their evilness and shown the righteous path of truth."

"Your truth."

"There is no other. If they do not come to see the truth, they must be… excised like the cancer they are so the body of the faithful can be whole again."

"One cannot be excised if one never belonged."

"All belong. They just do not understand yet."

"And if they never do?"

"They must be removed so the faithful may flourish."

"And the faithful are…?"

"Those who follow the law as given by God."

"Have you spoken to God?"

"No! You blaspheme heretic! No one can speak to the Almighty."

"Then how were the laws given to you?"

"Through the teachings of our most Revered Leader."

"Ah. So your leader talked with God."

"Yes. It is so written."

"But you just said that no one may talk with the Almighty."

"You dog! You dare question what is written?!"

"Yes. Was your leader not human like the rest of us?"

"Our Revered Leader was touched by the hand of God. The Leader's mouth moved but it was God who spoke. The Leader's hand wrote but it was God who made it so. Our Revered Leader was an instrument of God, no longer truly human, being touched by the divine."

"How do you know?"

"Curséd one! It is so written. As it is written, so it must be."

"And who wrote these things?"

"They come from the hand of our Revered Leader and those who adhere to those words."

"But there are other words, written by other hands, all in the name of God. What of them?"

"They are wrong. God has only spoken to the Revered Leader. All else are mistaken, deceived, or liars. Only our faith is the true one."

"And all else is anathema?"

"Yes. All else is against the will of God and must be removed."

"What then of the birds?"

"Birds?"

"Yes, the birds."

"They do not matter."

"Are they not God's creatures?"

"Yes. Yes. But what has that got to do with this?"

"Are they not a testament to the greatness of God?"

"Yes. Yes of course. But what…"

"What name do they use when they speak of God amongst themselves?"

"Speak of God! They do not speak of God. They do not speak. They are just beasts placed here by God to please us."

"Are you so sure?"

"Yes. Of course. It is…"

"so written. Yes. I know. How else could such a thing be?"

"Yes! Yes. You begin to see."

"No. I do not. The birds and the beasts all know God in their way. Yet they do not proselytize. They do not say,

'The Sparrow God is the only true God.' or 'The paw prints of the Creator tell us this and guide us on our way.' They are content to know that they exist. That God has made it so that they may live the life they have until the next may come.

They do not sit and squabble over meaningless things like ritual or tradition or clothing or how to pray or which prayers are better, truer than the rest.

They are born. They live. They mate. They have little ones. They grow old and die. They simply exist until they do not.

Are we really any different than they? Are these words you speak of truly a reason for war, for the punishment of others, for the extermination of those who question them or believe what is written elsewhere?"

"Yes."

"Yes? How can you say that? How can you be so simplistic?"

"I am protected by the armor of God. The words of our Revered Leader give me sustenance and meaning and show the way to goodness, true mercy, and eternal peace."

"Even though they are… mistaken?"

"But they are not."

"How do you know that?"

"Because it is so written."

"And all who do not so believe must be destroyed."

"Yes. Do you not see?"

"No. I do not."

"And that, heretic, is why you must die."

Silence came as both looked upon the other, one strong in faith, one in understanding. Finally the heretic spoke again.

"Then I shall pray for you while I have breath to do so."

For a moment, each gazed upon the other as the silence built to an almost physical presence full of a mix of sadness, resignation, and perhaps regret. At last there was a sound, like a sigh, too long held within, finally released. The scraping of hinges followed as the door was closed. And with that, the darkness was complete once more.

Thoughts Cast Upon
the Face of Eternity

There, I heard it once again, a breaking of a twig not far
away amidst this shifting span of forest where, but
moments past, I glimpsed the lingering shape of summer. It
has vanished now, taking the warmth and sunshine with it,
leaving me beneath a canopy of scattered scraps. Listen.
The wind of change blows to sweep the past away. It serves
as harbinger that chills me to my bones causing unwelcome
thoughts of what yet lies ahead.

The past is gone with tomorrow yet unformed. They are
both, just there, beyond my current reach and I could waste
a lifetime yearning for them to be other than they are.

But I will not think on this. This time is as important as any
other I might have. The sun still shines revealing, to all
who see, this world in all its glory. Now is the time for
now. Live and rejoice, come what may, for today is the
only time we live.

What is man but a fragment of reality? What shape is worn
is immaterial to the substance within. Thus a thousand
times a thousand times may we live. Yet each day is
precious, for each day is unique as is the shape that lives it.
Weaving the fabric of our lives from threads of our
imaginings, reality is as we see it to be. One's triumph is
another's disaster. One's hope is another's dream. One's
fact is but another's passing fancy.

Though we may live a million times, each life is precious in
its living. Savor each breath and taste the power of emotion
as the force of life moves within. Know reality in the
moment, in the instant of its passing. Know the sun as it

shines and the dark when sun has gone. Feel pain and joy and sorrow, and do not spurn the knowing of them, for each is a celebration of living. Though we grieve, we live and will do so again.

Hunger not for what was, for what is is as important. Know the past by the future and the future by the past. They are the same. Love and love will be returned. Shine and the light will be reflected in a thousand hearts that hunger for it. In all the moments we have lived, it is now that is the most important, for it is now that we live.

Let the woods change. Let the seasons come and go. Experience each change in its time and know the fullness of the moment. Live and, in the living, rejoice.

Prayer of the Discontent

I called in the valleys, but you were not there.

I looked through the sky, but I could not find you.

Where have you gone that I searched in vain?

Where can you be that you do not answer me?

What am I to think if you are not here?

Who am I to trust if you will not respond?

Does the wind blow less gently? No, it gently blows.

Does the sun warm me less? No, it warms my skin and lights the way.

The wind smoothed the ragged edges of the summer's heat, but you smoothed the jagged edges of my soul.

The sun warmed my skin, but you warmed my heart.

Where have you gone that I cannot see you?

What have I done that I am left among the lost?

You were my light.

You were the sun in my day.

You brightened the heavens and my heart, but you are gone.

Were you ever there?

Are love and understanding just shields to make this world seem better than it is?

I may give of myself, share what I have, and help others who have less, but is that truly important? What do the cares and needs of others matter if my cares and needs are met?

What does it matter that I exist in fear and hatred if I gain the things I want?

I grasp at truth and failing, accept the world and its reality as my own. But is this all there is? And if it is, what does it matter what I do?

I stand upon this world in watchful waiting, knowing that I see but fragments of the greater whole.

Yet truth is always there, if we choose to see.

And knowing such, what do I do?

What should I do?

Dialogue

"What should I do?" He asked to no one in particular as he passed the church. He was somewhat surprised then when he received an answer.

"Live. Enjoy yourself. Be happy."

"That's all?"

"That's all."

"But that's so easy."

"Easy?"

"There's no rules, no strictures, no don't do this or that."

"Uh huh."

"What's the catch?"

"Catch?"

"Yes. The catch. There's always a catch. Something that prevents you from doing what you want to do."

"Free will."

"Free will? That's the catch? How can free will be the catch?"

"Choices."

"Choices? What do you mean by tha… No wait. I know this one."

"Go on."

"Our choices determine how we live our lives. Whether we enjoy ourselves and whether we're happy."

"Very good."

"But how do we know what the right choices are?"

"It's a matter of perspective."

"Perspective? I don't think I follow you. You'll have to explain this one."

"Look at it this way. Perhaps for the most part there are no right or wrong choices… only choices and the consequences that come with them."

"No right or wrong?"

"Uh huh."

"Only consequences."

"Well not only consequences for these consequences may well determine the course of your life…"

"And whether I enjoy myself…"

"or find happiness."

"But that's tough."

"Is it?"

"That means I have to weigh each choice against the consequence that may follow."

"Perhaps. But you can never know all the consequences of your choices."

"But if I don't know the consequences, how can I choose?"

"Acceptance."

"Acceptance?"

"Accept that no choice is perfect. Accept that no one can know everything. Accept that choices must be made, that all futures are equally valid, but only one can occur at one time, with the understanding that you can live as you wish, enjoy the life you lead, and be happy as you do so."

"Based on choice."

"Yes."

"Founded on free will."

"Yes."

"So… what should I do?"

Belief

Belief is an armor against the truth.
No one is so blind as one who believes
their truth is all there is,
that their conception of the universe
is the governing one,
that all else must bow to their view,
their teachings,
their understanding of what exists
and what does not.

If there is one,
they are but a fanatic.

Ten, and they are a cult.

Hundreds compose a following.

Thousands make up a religion.

Millions begin a crusade
that endures
until they
or competing beliefs
are expunged from the world.

The Heavens Wept

The heavens wept
at the sight of ordinary men
in extraordinary times
leaving their homes
and lives behind
to serve the common good,
mortgaging their futures,
their hopes and dreams,
so that their families,
their sons and daughters,
parents and wives,
could live secure
and safe from harm
far from the pain
and anguish
that accompanies the thousand ways
a man can die
even if he survives
the immediate battle,
the urgency of the moment,
the despair
that comes with imminent defeat
and the joy
amidst the bone numbing tiredness
when he is still after all alive
when all around
have fallen into still repose
from which they shall not rise again.

They fall by the thousands
and the tens of thousands
but for each who falls
there comes another to carry on,
to persevere in the face of horror,

in the face of loss
profound and deep
as brothers bound by hardship,
joined by adversity,
lose their kin
in quick ways
and in slow
throughout the gathering twilight,
throughout the lingering days
of choking dust
and sucking mud,
of endless sun
and unceasing rain,
of noisome life
and quiet death.

In the end,
the carnage
claims more than any can know.
Hopes crushed,
dreams dashed
upon the field of battle,
souls battered
by visions of a world
twisted by the need to survive,
the imperative to persevere,
to achieve victory
in the name of a greater good,
without which all is lost,
without which
there is no dream to return to,
without which
the agony of war,
borne by the watchful dead
and the present living,
would not be worth the cost in time,

would not be worth the cost in resources,
would not be worth the cost in blood
split upon the waiting earth,
spent to purchase fleeting things,
a way of life,
a culture unbowed and unbending,
with things the way they were before,
before the price was known,
before the world was changed
by the act of saving it,
all sides
acting according to their righteous claims,
all done with the thought
that tomorrow will be better than today,
that their cause is just,
and that the enemy
must be stopped at any cost
to keep it so.

Some would say
the price is too high
and they would be correct.
The loss of one
is more cost than any
should be willing to bear,
the loss of ten
a burden to the soul,
the loss of thousands
an ever-present hemorrhage,
the loss of millions
unspeakable
in its impact on the future
present when combat is done,
the issue settled,
the cost tallied,
and the price paid.

And if there are victors,
they will praise their God
for their victory
and write the history
so that the future
will remember their past,
their reasons,
and the right of it,
to justify why it was needful,
to justify the loss
of those ordinary men
in extraordinary times
as the earth waited,
the dead watched,
and the heavens wept.

Epilog

Now that you have read these words and think you understand, you may choose to follow one of several paths.

You might become a hermit or live a monastic, simple life for the act of living is what is important, the rest is but trappings.

You might try to save the world for if we are all one then whatever you do to improve the lives of others improves your life when you are them.

You might try to experience everything that the world has to offer. For if choice is what expands existence, then you must make as many choices as possible, experience all that you can now for next time you will forget and choose differently.

You might try to gather as much power, wealth, importance, material things, etcetera, to yourself as possible. For if we are all one and will live those other lives of deprivation, poverty, sickness, pain, sorrow, and despair, then you might as well get everything you can in this life now.

You might live a life as a libertine following a hedonistic existence experiencing every pleasure possible. For if you are doomed to live those other lives, then you might as well enjoy yourself now.

You might hunker down and live a conservative, safe life seeing this time as a reprieve, a rest period from all the rest.

You might live your life as best you can, understanding but adapting that knowledge to the simple and complex challenges that each life brings.

You might understand and pretend that you don't so you may hide from your self and live a life sheltered by others' rules and justified by traditions, culture, and religious teachings.

You may read this and snort in disbelief and go your way to live as you damn well please seemingly immune to the calls of convention and the strictures of society.

Now that you have read this, which path or combination of them will you choose? Or will you find another way? In any event, regardless of the path, be careful out there.

Acceptance

I don't understand it.
Don't know if I ever will.
But I've come to accept it.
Come to accept that
there are some things
beyond my ability to grasp,
beyond my ability to see clearly,
beyond my ability to control.

It isn't so much that I've changed.
Everyone does in the course of time.
It's more that I've come to appreciate
that I am the center of some things
but not all things,
that not every thing has to be shaped
to suit my purpose,
that each plays its own role
in the scheme of things
often on a level
beyond my view,
beyond my experience,
beyond my comprehension
and that it is OK
for that to be so.

Postscript

One day, when I was a small child, I went into the woods behind the house. It was one of those perfect days, breeze blowing gently through the leaves of the trees, sky an azure blue, and sun making everything vivid and distinct.

As I stood there and looked around, it all became clear. I could see everything, hear everything. I knew everything and "THE ANSWER" was there, just there in front of me. It was wonderful to comprehend the essence of existence.

A pity that I couldn't remember it later…

It takes an instant to know,
a lifetime to truly understand,
an eternity to accomplish

The Book of Light

List of Illustrations

1. Midnight Sun: Photo art by Pat Grieco   8

2. Event/Choice Function Wave:
Illustration by Pat Grieco   21

3. Parallel and Multiverses:
Illustration by Pat Grieco   24

4. Meta-universe Space Time Environment:
Illustration by Pat Grieco   25

The Book of Light

ABOUT THE AUTHOR

Born and raised in a small rural town, the author left to
pursue higher education and a career which took him to
different parts of the world. After a lifetime listening to the
whisper of the wind, the burble of a brook, and the sound of
songbirds all imparting their wisdom, he's returned to his
roots, spending his days as a country gentleman, taking the
time now and then to put some words on paper.